THE TINY GARDEN

F

FRANCES LINCOLN LIMITED
PUBLISHERS
www.franceslincoln.com

THE T

GA

ON

Below Tightly packed containers and a bench transform a narrow strip of concrete into a proper garden.

could be a long flowering season, good autumn colour, fruits you can eat or blooms you can pick.

The final section of the book provides you with all the information you need to keep the garden looking its best. The important thing to remember is that gardening, on this scale at any rate, is actually quite easy. All plants want to grow, so if you give them the right conditions they will reward you for months or even years on end. Many pests and diseases can be deterred simply by buying healthy plants and keeping them well fed, watered and clear of garden debris.

About the plant lists Throughout the book, plants are recommended for various purposes. These are only a tiny selection and in most cases many others would also be suitable. If a variety is mentioned then it is particularly recommended; if not, any within the species could probably be chosen (but check that trees and shrubs will not grow too large for the space).

To help you choose suitable plants, the lists are divided into trees, shrubs, perennials, biennials, annuals and bulbs. Bear in mind that there is considerable crossover between the groups. Small trees such as holly may behave more like shrubs, for example, and a large shrub such as spindle (*Euonymus*) may perform the same function as a tree. Many short-lived perennials are better grown as annuals (as in the case of morning glory, *Ipomoea tricolor*) or as biennials (as in the case of sweet William, *Dianthus barbatus*). Many plants commonly listed as annuals are actually perennials (such as snapdragon, *Antirrhinum*) and may last for several years if happily situated.

GETTING STARTED

Before you begin to create a tiny garden it is worth spending a little time evaluating the pros and cons of your site, even if you are simply planning a few changes to an already mature garden. This chapter highlights factors, such as the type of soil or the level of exposure to sun and wind, which may affect your garden design, and it also suggests some ways of planning a garden in a very limited space. Many of the topics covered here are explored in greater detail later in the book.

It is often easiest to start by making a plan. Using graph paper and ink, plot the exact dimensions of the site, including the position of doors and windows and relevant features of the garden's surroundings, such as good or bad views and overhanging plants. Mark heights, slopes and changes of level and note which way walls face as this will influence where you put plants; as a general rule, a south-facing wall will be the sunniest (for more information see page 71). Then sketch in your ideas, using pencil so that you can try out variations without erasing the basic dimensions. You may also find one of the garden-design computer programs useful; some show what the garden will look like at different times of year and the effect that will be created as the plants grow.

Most houses are surrounded by pipes, drains, manhole covers and a whole host of other unsightly features. These should be marked on the plan, along with possible solutions. It is obviously not a good idea to pave over a manhole cover but you could cover one with a container, a trailing plant such as ivy or a paving stone in a removable frame. Pipes are not sturdy enough to be used as plant supports, but can be disguised with climbing plants trained over trellis. If you need the space for drying clothes, you can fix a retractable washing line to a wall and wind it up when not in use. Dustbins may be another unattractive necessity which, if you have room, could be hidden in a shallow lean-to shed. This may be painted and screened with containers.

If you are working with a roof, balcony or window ledge you may need a professional survey to establish how much weight the site can support. Remember that containers full of soil are heavy and also that plants grow; your perfectly shaped shrub may be the size of a small tree in a few years and will put corresponding pressure on its supports.

Boundaries and views It is a good idea to consider the boundaries of your garden and any views at the planning stage. You can put up or take down fences, walls and hedges, but check for any legal restrictions which may apply. (You may need permission to alter a boundary marker and in some areas, such as housing estates, it is illegal to erect barriers over a certain height.)

Don't despair if you cannot change the boundary itself as you may be able to change the impression it makes by altering its colour. Pale walls will give an increased sense of space and light. A neutral shade may be a more practical long-term choice than white,

Below A roof garden is an oasis of calm in the heart of the city. This row of containers is just high enough to provide shelter from the traffic and passers-by.

which can quickly turn an unappetizing shade of grey. Soft, sandy yellows and beiges complement most plants without dominating them. Alternatively, use a strong colour to emphasize a wall or feature.

If you live in a town you will almost certainly overlook, or be overlooked by, other properties or their gardens. There is little you can do to avoid this, but it is usually possible to hide an unsightly prospect by growing plants over a trellis screen. This will allow through a certain amount of air and light, but disguise the view beyond. If you are overlooked from above it may be possible to build a simple frame or pergola and train plants over it. This will provide a beautiful canopy which does not block out the light. In both cases a wire frame could be used instead of wood, creating a less solid screen but allowing through more light. (See page 72 for more on the great variety of climbing plants available).

Exposure to light and wind Another factor to consider is the amount of light and wind the site receives and whether this will vary with the seasons. In summer the sun will be higher and you may get a great deal more sunshine than in winter, when surrounding buildings may cast shadows. High window sills and balconies may receive a lot of sunlight depending on the direction they face (south-facing sites receive the most, north-facing the least), but they will also be more exposed to the elements. This is particularly true of roof gardens, which receive maximum light and maximum wind exposure. Lower gardens may

get less sun, but may also be more sheltered. An enclosed garden can be several degrees warmer than the surrounding area and this will extend the range of plants you can grow.

You can improve an exposed site by providing shelter (see page 57), but there is less you can do if your space if very dark. Fortunately, there are plants for every situation; see page 59 for wind- and

drought-tolerant plants and page 63 for plants that will thrive in shady situations.

Types of soil If you are only using pots you will be able to choose your own soil, but if there is already a bed it may be worth using a simple pH tester from the garden centre to establish whether the soil is acid or alkaline. A reading of 7 is neutral; anything above is alkaline and anything below is acid. In fact, only a few plants are fussy about the pH of the soil, especially heathers and rhododendrons which will not thrive unless grown in acid conditions. *Hydrangea macrophylla* needs acid soil to produce its distinctive blue flowers.

It is a good idea to find out whether your soil is predominantly clay or sand, or, ideally, a loamy mixture of the two. Do this by handling the soil and testing how quickly it drains. Clay will feel smooth and slightly slippery, and will drain slowly if you dig a hole and fill it with water. Sand drains much more quickly, and can be identified by its gritty feel. Again, many plants will not be affected by the type of soil, but some do have specific drainage requirements.

Don't despair if your only flowerbed has soil that is unsuitable for the one plant you really want to grow. Soil with too much sand or clay can be improved by digging in organic material or adding grit. Alternatively, you could always grow the plant in a large pot or even simply change the entire soil. This would not be feasible in a large garden, but on a tiny scale importing a few bags of the right soil

would not be too expensive. This option is well worth considering if the soil is full of rubble and builders' rubbish. (See pages 133–4 for more on improving soil.)

Designing a tiny garden Once you have evaluated the pros and cons of the site, you can consider the possibilities for change. One of the advantages of gardening on a tiny scale is that you can make alterations that would be prohibitively expensive in a larger garden. You can erect a new fence or wall, remove existing plants or, as discussed, change the entire soil in a flowerbed. You could even give the garden a completely new look by changing the ground surface, digging up or laying concrete or paving stones (for some ideas, see 'Patios', page 22).

Books, magazines, gardening shows and other gardens are all good sources of inspiration, even if you only use part of the design. The following section, 'Design solutions for tiny spaces', will also show you a selection of different styles for tiny gardens and suggest ideas for particular situations. Treat them as starting points rather than fixed plans, and mix and match the various designs (an idea for a light well may work just as well in a passageway and many suggestions for roofs and balconies are interchangeable).

It will help if you make a list of things that need to be accommodated in your space as well as features that you'd like to have. The list might include: plant containers; table and chairs; wall, fence or trellis for privacy; a large feature shrub or tree; water feature; lighting; play area for children; bicycles and dustbins; space for compost, dormant plants and seeds; lean-to shed or other storage area. Some of these features may at first glance seem more at home in a large garden, but it is possible to fit any of them into a tiny space. A children's play area, for example, could mean a small paddling pool on a balcony, which will keep young children amused on a hot day,

can be used to cool adult feet in the evening and will fold away into a cupboard when not in use. You won't be able to include all the items in a tiny garden, so decide on your top priority and work from there.

An illusion of size There is a rule of thumb that to create the illusion of greater size you should divide your garden into smaller spaces. This may be true, but it will be impossible to divide a really tiny garden in this way. The solution is to provide several distinct focal points that will trick the eye into perceiving the space as larger than it really is. A row of pots along one side of a long, narrow passageway can be monotonous; it would be better to arrange the containers in clusters, perhaps with a single eye-catching pot on the opposite side. A change in level, achieved through a small raised bed for example, will also create an illusion of size.

Another useful rule is 'less is more'. A few large features are usually more effective than several smaller ones. A single decent-sized flowerbed will create more impact than a series of very thin ones and will leave you room to position an ornament or a table and chairs against a wall that might not be so well suited to growing plants. 'Less is more' does not mean the garden should have less in it, but that it should not contain too many different things. A variety of plants will usually look better if their containers are in some way linked, possibly by material or colour. Equally, a variety of containers can be brought together by a simple planting scheme.

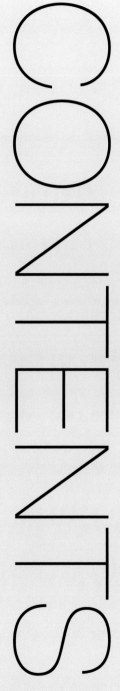

CONTENTS

6 INTRODUCTION

8 GETTING STARTED

14 DESIGN SOLUTIONS FOR TINY SPACES
16 FRONT GARDENS
22 PATIOS
28 FLOWERBEDS
32 PASSAGES
36 LIGHT WELLS & BASEMENTS
42 BALCONIES
46 ROOFS
52 STEPS

54 PLANTING IDEAS
56 EXPOSED PLACES
60 SHADY PLOTS
64 OVERLOOKED AREAS
68 POLLUTED SITES
70 WALLS
74 SEASONAL INTEREST

80 PUTTING IDEAS INTO PRACTICE
82 PLANTS FOR A TINY GARDEN
90 LAWNS & GROUND COVER
94 CONTAINERS
102 HERBS, FRUIT & VEGETABLES
108 WATER FEATURES
114 FURNITURE, LIGHTING & ORNAMENT
124 WALLS, FENCES AND TRELLIS

130 KEEP YOUR GARDEN LOOKING GOOD
132 MAINTAINING A TINY GARDEN
132 TOOLS FOR A TINY GARDEN
133 PREPARING THE SOIL AND PLANTING
134 PLANTS OR SEEDS?
134 PLANTING TREES AND SHRUBS
134 PLANTING PERENNIALS, BIENNIALS AND ANNUALS
135 WATERING, MULCHING AND FEEDING
136 COMPOSTING
136 PRUNING, TRAINING AND WEEDING
138 DEALING WITH PESTS AND DISEASES

141 INDEX
144 ACKNOWLEDGMENTS

No space is too tiny for a garden. In comparison with some gardens in the countryside, almost any town or suburban garden will be considered tiny; and from the same point of view the gardens in this book are practically non-existent. Yet wonderful gardens can be created in passages, light wells and basements; on stairways, window ledges and flat roofs – in other words, in the leftover spaces of a building that are usually ignored or used as a dumping ground for dustbins or bicycles. In fact, however small or dark it is, any area that is open to the sky can be converted into a garden.

Designing a tiny garden is much easier than you might think. Much depends on common sense. The most important thing to bear in mind is that you are creating a garden, not simply plonking down a group of pots. Once you look at the space in this way its possibilities become much greater. The top of the fire escape may only be a few square feet but if you think creatively you may be able to fit in a couple of chairs and three decent-sized decorative containers with climbers – and suddenly you have created a miniature garden. It is also perfectly possible to make a very rewarding garden that you look at, rather than go into. A single window box will transform the view from a room and can be used for growing both decorative and culinary plants.

Don't be bound by conventional constraints if you want an original theme. Part of the charm of gardening is that almost anything goes: this is your garden and it should please you. What is crucial is that you ensure every detail contributes to the effect you want to achieve. In a tiny garden, the whole area will be in view of the house and on show all the time, so you won't be able to get away with the unsightly features that could be hidden or ignored in a larger garden. One of the advantages of a tiny space, however, is that it will only take a little time and effort to keep the whole place looking perfect.

The purpose of this book is to enable you to create a garden wherever you live. The first section shows how to plan the area, balancing its possibilities with your needs and preferences. The second section looks at design solutions for particular situations to help you to make the most of your own space. There is considerable crossover between the different areas, so if you have a balcony, for example, you can pick and choose ideas from the chapter on roofs as well as the one on balconies.

It is unlikely that a tiny garden will offer ideal conditions for all the plants you want to grow. The third section recommends a selection of suitable plants for problem areas as well as possible solutions, such as making a windy site more sheltered or enlivening a dark area with plants that thrive in shade.

The fourth section explains how to put your ideas into practice and covers every aspect of a garden, from plants and containers to lighting and water features. Everything in a tiny garden has to justify the space it occupies. Your plants, for example, should always offer at least two interesting features, which

**TO BARRY, WHO INSPIRED ME
TO LOVE THE GARDEN I HAVE**

Frances Lincoln Ltd
4 Torriano Mews
Torriano Avenue
London NW5 2RZ
www.franceslincoln.com

The Tiny Garden
Copyright © Frances Lincoln Ltd 2006
Text copyright © Jane McMorland Hunter 2006

British Library Cataloguing in Publication data
A catalogue record for this book is available from
the British Library

First Frances Lincoln edition: 2006

ISBN 978-0-7112-2813-9

Printed and bound in Singapore by Star Standard

9 8 7 6 5 4 3 2 1

Designer Caroline Clark
Editor Fiona Robertson
Picture editor Sue Gladstone

Left Simple furniture and leafy containers make a tiny terrace the perfect spot for eating out.

Below This plain white canopy lets in light at the same time as it gives the seating area privacy.

Plan a small space for the overall effect. If you only have room for a few plants, try for a selection that will work all year round. A tiny garden is going to be right next to the house, so even if you don't actually go outside during winter the plants will be visible through the windows. A single evergreen, such as a viburnum, in a tub will require virtually no maintenance, provide an interesting view in winter and act as a backdrop for more colourful flowers in summer.

Transferring the plan to the garden It is worth leaving any established planting for as long as possible as many bulbs and perennials die down in their dormant period and during this time may not be easy to recognize. Before you pull up existing plants consider whether they have been put there for a reason. Shrubs can act as a barrier against wind and noise, and the large tree that shades your garden may also provide privacy or block an unattractive view.

Remember also that you do not need to complete the design in one go. As the plants grow the garden will gradually evolve and you may well change your mind about how you want it to develop. The plan can easily be adapted as you proceed.

Once you are satisfied that your plan will work within the constraints of the space, transfer it to the garden using string and stones as markers. You will probably make further alterations, but this initial plan will provide helpful guidelines to what you can fit in. If it feels overcrowded you may have to reassess your priorities and jettison anything that doesn't work.

Leave the plan for at least a week and check it at different times of day. Does the design make the most of the light? Is the seating in the best position? Are you satisfied with the overall effect? This may seem a lot of trouble for an area the size of a pocket handkerchief, but now is the time to discover the possibilities, not when the furniture you ordered turns up at the door. And when you are happy with the plan, you can set about creating the tiny garden of your dreams.

DESIG
SOLU
FOR
SPAC

Front gardens tend to be more functional than back gardens or balconies and are on show all year round. They serve as a barrier between your house and the pavement or road, accommodate dustbins and possibly bicycles or even a car, and, most importantly, provide access to your front door. This last point must be remembered when you are planning the garden. A mass of containers with spreading plants may look wonderful, but will soon become irritating if it blocks the path or doorway.

It depends to some extent on where you live, but the likelihood is that prime requirements for your front garden will be privacy and security. In many ways plants can provide a better barrier than a tall fence or wall: they will allow light to filter through rather than blocking it out totally, and they will provide seasonal interest. If you want to discourage people from coming into the garden, you can always plant prickly shrubs such as berberis, pyracantha and roses.

A thick hedge will provide the most privacy. Yew, box, bay and holly will produce a dense, attractive hedge, but all are slow growing and it will be several years before they make a decent screen. Hornbeam and beech grow into thick, solid hedges and although their leaves change colour in the autumn they do not usually drop until the new growth pushes through in the spring. They will take up less space than the faster growing, but more invasive, Western red cedar (*Thuja plicata*) and privet.

An alternative to a solid barrier is a selection of shrubs that create an informal screen. Shrubby honeysuckle (*Lonicera nitida* 'Baggesen's Gold'), daphne (*D. odora* 'Aureomarginata') and Mexican orange blossom (*Choisya ternata* 'Sundance') all have beautiful leaves and will brighten the garden throughout the year. If you live on a busy road it is worth choosing specimens that will not mind a degree of pollution. Escallonia, hawthorn, elaeagnus, *Osmanthus* x *burkwoodii*, rosemary and all the plants listed in 'Plants for polluted sites' (page 69) will thrive regardless of the fumes.

Formal styles are effective in front gardens as long as they are well maintained. Clipped box or bay in matching pots flanking the front door can create an imposing entrance. Topiary is expensive, however; a cheaper way of creating a similar effect is to train ivy over a shaped metal frame. Ivy plants can be bought cheaply and will grow quickly to cover the frame.

If you are concerned that expensive containers and topiary are vulnerable to theft they can be cemented to the ground (make sure you do not block the drainage holes) or secured with a chain. An alternative is to plant a single specimen and surround it with paving or gravel. Evergreens tend to be less hardy than deciduous plants, but they will look good all year and should be sheltered by the house. You can add seasonal colour by arranging bulbs and annuals around the main plant.

A less formal arrangement can be more welcoming, especially if you use soft-leaved plants

DENS

18

Below Topiary will lend year-round colour and a touch of formality to the tiniest space.

Right Even the pavement in front of a house is a potential garden. Here, Virginia creeper (*Parthenocissus quinquefolia*) on the wall provides a backdrop for potted plants.

and gentle colours. A good base of shrubs might be hebe (*H.* 'Great Orme'), *Convolvulus cneorum*, weigela (*W. florida* 'Foliis Purpureis', *W.* 'Florida Variegata'), artemisia (*A. absinthium* 'Lambrook Silver', *A.* 'Powis Castle') and lavender (*Lavandula angustifolia* and *L. stoechas*), with hollyhocks, foxgloves and Japanese anemones growing up in between.

Climbers such as jasmine (*Jasminum officinale, J.* x *stephanense*) or honeysuckle (*Lonicera* x *americana, L.* x *heckrottii, L. periclymenum* 'Belgica', *L.p.* 'Serotina') can be trained around the door or encouraged to grow up the front of the house on a framework of wires. Other beautiful climbers are wisteria or repeat-flowering roses – *Rosa* 'Gloire de Dijon' (apricot), *R.* 'Maigold' (yellow), *R.* 'New Dawn' (pale pink), *R.* 'Pink Perpétué' (rose pink) or *R.* 'Zéphirine Drouhin' (deep pink), all of which will thrive regardless of the aspect (see 'Walls', page 70, for more on climbing plants). Hanging baskets or wall-mounted pots will give height to the garden.

If you have a wall along the street side of the garden you could construct a raised bed, which would be much easier to look after than a row of containers. It is not advisable to site a raised bed along the house walls because of the damp, but as long as you incorporate drainage holes it will do a free-standing wall no harm (see page 30). Taking advantage of the extra height the bed provides, you could create an open screen using tall perennials and annuals such as sunflowers, hollyhocks, *Verbena bonariensis,* Japanese anemones, morning glory and sweet peas trained up wigwams and canes. This display would die down in winter but small shrubs could fill the gaps. Bergenia and hellebores will add interest in winter and early spring. If you also plant bulbs for the spring, the bed will look good all year round, the shrubs providing a permanent structure around which perennials, bulbs and annuals can grow.

Don't forget about scented plants. Many winter-flowering shrubs, such as daphne (*D. odora, D.o.* 'Aureomarginata') and viburnum (*V. tinus* 'Eve Price'), are highly scented and work well in a front garden where you can appreciate the fragrance on a daily basis as you walk past. Lilacs (*Syringa meyeri* 'Palibin', *S. pubescens* subsp. *patula* 'Miss Kim') have a short flowering season, but are worth growing just for their beautiful scent. Wonderfully fragrant annuals and perennials include tobacco plants, sweet peas and sweet rocket (*Hesperis matronalis*). If the space is sunny you could grow aromatic herbs as well. (See page 88 for more on plants to grow for fragrance.)

The material used to edge a tiny garden becomes as much a part of the space as the plants. Create a country cottage effect with roses such as *Rosa* 'New Dawn' (seen here on the wall) and white pickets, or use iron railings to produce a more imposing style, or paint palings a striking shade to complement the colours of a herb garden.

PATIOS

f you are reading this book, the chances are your patio is your entire garden rather than just part of it. This means that all of it has to look great, including the ground surface. This should be hard wearing, level, properly drained and attractive. Depending on your taste and budget there are a number of options available.

Bricks Old brick is beautiful, particularly if your space is sunny, but may make a shady patio darker still. If you want a smoother effect modern bricks are usually more even, and sometimes paler. You can use bricks to create a pattern (such as a circular or herringbone design) or emphasize the shape of the space: laid lengthwise bricks will make the patio seem longer; laid sideways they will make it seem wider.

Stone slabs Stone paving ranges from natural stone to multicoloured reconstituted slabs. As you are only paving a small area you may be able to afford a more expensive stone. Traditional stone slabs look wonderful, but can be slippery when wet. At the other end of the scale, very cheap paving may appear to be a bargain but is often brittle and prone to cracking. There is a huge range in between, and you can create almost any effect you want. If choosing coloured paving, be careful that it does not dominate the patio, as everything from furniture to plants will need to tone in with the colour you have chosen.

Slate paving can look amazing, particularly when surrounded by silvery plants such as artemisia (*A. absinthium* 'Lambrook Silver', *A.* 'Powis Castle') and rabbit's ears (*Stachys byzantina*). Slate tends to darken a space, however, and can also be slippery when wet.

Granite setts These square stones create an interesting textured surface, but are very hard to get flat. They can also work out expensive to lay as each one is so small. It is possible to buy larger paving slabs shaped to look like setts, which can be laid with much less labour.

Tiles These come in a huge range of colours, textures and sizes. Always use tiles designed specifically for outdoor use and make sure that they are frost proof. They are particularly useful for garden design, whether you are laying a strip of mosaic, transforming your patio into a Moorish courtyard or using terracotta for a warm Mediterranean feel.

Concrete A useful material that will fit any space, concrete can be dyed or mixed with aggregates to give a more interesting texture. If the whole space is concrete it may be worth digging up part of it to make a flowerbed, constructing a raised bed on top or using it as a base for more attractive paving or tiles.

Gravel This comes in a range of colours and differently sized stones and has the advantage of easily filling any space. However, it must be laid on a solid base or your garden furniture will sink into it.

Below, left Varied surface materials – metal gridwork, wooden decking, stone paving – define different areas in this tiny garden. The spears of *Astelia chathamica* and the large, spreading pinnate leaves of *Melianthus major* add variety of form to the planting.

Below, right Mellow paving combines with relaxed planting and the gentle plash of water to create a haven of peace in a city garden.

Right A large mirror on the wall reflects the tiny formal garden that has been carefully composed in this tiled courtyard.

Decking Timber comes in a wide range of colours and, like bricks, can be laid to emphasize the length or width of your patio. All timber must be initially treated with preservative and will need regular cleaning and possibly repeat applications of preservative. Moss can look charming on bricks, but will do nothing to enhance a decked patio. Scrubbing with a weak solution of bleach should deter weeds and moss, but the wood may need retreating with preservative or repainting afterwards. Decking tends to be slippery when wet.

Once you have decided on the patio's surface, the next aspect to consider is the plants. If possible leave at least one area where plants can grow directly in the ground rather than in containers. In a flowerbed, however tiny, plants will be better able to spread their roots and will require less watering. Even the smallest raised bed will, by introducing a change in level, make a patio garden seem more interesting and you can make a feature of the bed's retaining wall, using it as a seat and choosing bricks, treated timber, stone or concrete blocks to match

Left This high metal screen, installed for security and privacy, has been painted green and covered with plants so that it becomes part of the garden.

Below Wooden furniture like that shown on the left blends well into a natural environment, but if you really want to make a statement try teaming up unusual materials and shapes. In the garden shown on the right, the slick surface of an aluminium table contrasts with a gnarled old tree whose glass-covered branches shimmer in the sun.

the rest of the patio (see pages 30 and 50 for more information about raised beds).

Depending on the aspect, sun-loving jasmine (*Jasminum officinale, J.* x *stephanense*), ivy – which can be grown in any situation – or climbing roses could be trained from containers over the walls. *Rosa* 'Zéphirine Drouhin' is particularly good for small patios as it will thrive in shade, is virtually thornless and flowers repeatedly throughout the summer.

A group of three or four medium-sized pots can be rearranged with the seasons to ensure the best display of colour in a limited space. As the year progresses, spring bulbs and wallflowers could be followed by lilies, with a pelargonium filling the gap to winter. A small shrub, such as berberis or clipped box, will provide year-round interest. Larger containers could hold choisya, fuchsia and a rose such as *Rosa* 'Queen Mother', which has pink flowers from summer to autumn. Use bulbs and

annuals for seasonal interest. The largest containers, which will be heavy to move, can be reserved for a permanent display, while the smaller pots can be shifted around as the plants fade.

In a very restricted area like a patio, the furniture will be one of the main features of the garden, so take time to choose the right pieces. Stylish metal or wooden furniture is always an asset. Consider the shape of the patio when you are buying furniture. If you can fit it against a wall, a rectangular table will be more economical with space than a round one. You may also want some form of electric lighting, particularly if you plan to eat outside. Candlelight is beautiful, but more practical if supplemented by an electric light in the background. Position it carefully so that it illuminates the seating area only and creates an illusion of depth by leaving the rest of the patio in shadow. (See 'Furniture, lighting & ornament', page 114, for more suggestions.)

FLOWERBE

Above, left Cistus shrubs add a touch of pink to this planting in a circular patio, complementing the brightly coloured chairs.

Above, right Canes of phyllostachys, pitchers of sarracenia, spiky agave leaves and globe-headed *Allium cristophii* flourish in a contemporary garden.

Your garden may only consist of a single flowerbed but, if this is the case, you have an advantage over someone with room only for containers.

If you have an existing flowerbed, consider its position when buying plants as this will be the main factor in determining what grows best there (see page 72 for lists of plants for different positions). If you are creating a bed from scratch, make it as large as possible. One bigger bed is better than several tiny ones as it will give you more scope for planting and create a more impressive effect. You can use containers to provide pockets of interest in other corners of your space.

If you are dealing with just one bed, you can afford to ensure that the soil is top quality. Use bags of multi-purpose compost or a mixture of soil and compost. Even if the bed is full of plants the soil will be greatly improved if you dig in organic matter where you can and provide a mulch in spring.

If your flowerbed is tiny, concentrate on putting in a mixture of plants that provide a balance of interest for all seasons. Combining a permanent backdrop in the form of an evergreen climber such as variegated ivy with a shrub that offers good autumn colour and bulbs inserted in between summer-flowering plants will give you a colourful bed for most of the year (see 'Seasonal interest', page 74, for more suggestions).

If your site has a solid base (paving, concrete or impacted hardcore) you may be able to construct a raised bed by building a retaining wall and filling the

Far left Profuse green and white planting in raised beds and large containers provides a lush background for a minimalist patio.

Left Lilac-purple *Verbena bonariensis* on stiff, upright stems above mounds of purple *Lavandula angustifolia* and grey-leaved *Santolina chamaecyparissus*.

Below This tiny garden is so lavishly stocked with plants at varying heights that it's hardly possible to see the wall, let alone the neighbours. In the foreground trumpets of *Lilium regale* contrast with domed hydrangea flowerheads.

space with a good soil mixture. It can be worth doing this even if you already have a bed as an additional level will create the illusion of a larger space. You will also gain the scent of low-growing flowers, such as herbs, tobacco plants, night-scented stock (*Matthiola longipetala* subsp. *bicornis*) and scented-leaved geraniums – *Pelargonium* 'Attar of Roses' (rose-scented), *P.* 'Copthorne' (spicy), *P.* 'Lady Plymouth', *P.* 'Mabel Grey' (lemon), *P. tomentosum* (peppermint).

If possible break up the surface below the bed. If you can't do this, put down a 10cm/4in layer of pebbles or grit and create drainage holes every 15cm/6in along the base of the retaining wall to ensure that the bed does not become waterlogged. The retaining wall, whether made of bricks, stone or timber, must be strong enough to contain plants and soil. If you want to use it as a seat, reserve the front of the bed for tough plants that will not mind being sat on occasionally, such as thyme, sedum (*S. kamtschaticum, S. spathulifolium*) or low-growing campanulas (*C. carpatica, C. cochleariifolia, C. portenschlagiana, C. poscharskyana*).

Your flowerbed may be tiny but, depending on the amount of light available, there are plenty of possibilities. A sunny bed against a wall could become a miniature kitchen garden with an espalliered fruit tree, vegetables in the soil and herbs in a window box. Alternatively you could create a tropical feel in a shady space with a wall-mounted fountain and lush ferns (*Adiantum, Polystichum*).

Right An imaginative makeover of a dark passageway, in which ranked spheres of box (*Buxus sempervirens*) and ornamental pots on tall plinths provide contrasting shapes and textures and make the most of the available light.

PASSAGES

If you are planning to keep plants in a passage, the first point to consider is its function. You will have a lot more scope if it is not used for access. If people pass through regularly you will have to keep clear a strip of at least 1m/3ft. You also need to decide what you are going to do with any items, such as bins and bicycles, that are usually stored there (see page 115 for storage solutions).

Narrow passages tend to be dark. A coat of pale paint on the walls will immediately improve the area, as will the use of pale bricks, stone or gravel on the ground. Replacing solid fencing with trellis will allow through additional light. You can create a green roof by growing climbers over timbers or wires suspended across the path. This will make the area even darker, however; an alternative is an arch which will block out less light than a full trellis roof and, by breaking up the length, will make the space look more interesting. Pin trellis flat to create the vertical parts of the arch and fix a 30cm/12in-wide strip of trellis across the top. Suitable climbers for a shady environment are ivy, clematis and golden hop (*Humulus lupulus* 'Aureus').

The range of plants you can grow will depend on how much space and light you have. If the passage is wide enough, large containers will give you considerable latitude for planting. Climbers or trained wall shrubs are usually most suitable for passages, as they will not spread out and block the way. Euonymus, Japanese quince (*Chaenomeles speciosa*) and pyracantha can easily be trained to sit flat against a wall. Chocolate vine (*Akebia quinata*), clematis, ivy

Below A simple colour scheme including vibrant pelargoniums lends this passage a feeling of spaciousness, while a fake window adds the illusion of length.

(*Hedera*), roses (*Rosa*) and winter jasmine (*Jasminum nudiflorum*) will all climb neatly. If your passage is very dark you will have to rely on plants that thrive in shade, but there are plenty to choose from (see page 63 for suggestions).

If your passage is narrow use troughs rather than circular containers, as they hold more earth and take up less space, and move around small pots containing annuals or bulbs to give seasonal interest. Arranging the containers in one long line can be monotonous; cluster them in groups to break up the space and make it seem larger. You can fix half baskets and pots to the wall, where they will add colour and variety without using up valuable floor space. Though plastic pots are considered ugly, they are often the best choice of container for hanging as they weigh less than other materials and can easily be disguised with trailing plants.

The wider the passage, the greater your opportunities for design. Water bubbling from the spout of a wall-mounted fountain is a lovely way of catching the light and livening up the darkest corner. You could position a narrow table against one wall, with chairs and a light for eating out at night. Choose chairs that can be tucked under the table when not in use. If there is a window looking on to the passage, make sure the view from inside is also attractive. The window itself could be transformed into a colourful feature, with a box on the sill and climbers trained over trellis erected around the frame.

Below Pale walls and floor make the most of limited light and provide a simple backdrop for dramatic sculpture and a largely green planting, accented by tall white lilies, blue and white echinops, and white daisies.

LIGHT WELLS

The most important factor influencing your choice of plants for a light well or basement will be the amount of light it receives. On the plus side, many white-flowered plants such as choisya and viburnum will thrive. You can introduce colour on a seasonal basis with plants such as pulmonarias, tobacco plants and busy Lizzies, all of which live happily in a shady environment. However, grey- and silver-leaved plants do not do well in very dim conditions, and variegated species may become less brightly coloured.

Access may also be a limiting factor: if a light well is only accessible by climbing out of a window you will probably want plants that are as trouble-free as possible. Buy the largest container you can and plant *Fatsia japonica,* holly, ivy or bamboo (*Arundinaria* or *Phyllostachys*), all of which will provide year-round interest in return for virtually no maintenance. You will need to water the plants for the first couple of years until they are established and occasionally afterwards. They will also benefit from a feed in spring, but that is all – they won't even need pruning unless they get too large for the space.

If basement steps have to be kept clear of containers for access, you can train plants up the sides of the steps and walls. Use ivy as a backdrop with clematis (late-flowering Viticellas do not mind shade) or nasturtiums for interest. If the space has to accommodate bins and bicycles that are moved regularly, you could put up a low fence to divide the decorative and functional areas and shield the plants.

The main feature of a basement area or light well will be the walls, so it's a good idea to clean, repair and, if you wish, paint them. A shade of cream will lighten the area and lasts longer than white. You could put up trellis, either as decoration in itself or as a plant support. White or pale trellis will stand out against a dark wall, while brown or green will merge with the plants.

Walls can be used to support features such as containers, water spouts, mosaics or mirrors. The advantage of positioning a container part-way up the wall is that it will get that much more light, and you can have plants such as fuchsias growing up and trailers such as lobelia cascading down. You can position a mirror to create the impression of looking into another garden or even put up one that covers the width of one wall to double the space (see page 117 for more ideas).

To dispel the gloom, use sand-coloured slabs or gravel rather than grey paving or bricks, and choose containers in light or neutral shades. Artificial lighting can be used to good effect, either to spotlight a particular feature or architectural plant (see page 115) or to light the whole area.

Your decisions about the number and type of plants will determine the feel of the space. You can create a restrained, elegant look with a single tree or ivy and a statue, or you can transform the same area into a jungle with hart's tongue fern (*Asplenium scolopendrium* is pale green and *A.s.* Cristatum Group is darker with crinkled leaves), soft shield fern

Previous page A pristine snow-white décor and a splash of red cyclamen chase away gloom from a deep basement.

Left Dicksonia antarctica makes a dramatic statement.

This page, clockwise from top Mirrors and an overhead lamp bring light to a dark corner; buff is a warm choice of colouring for a background wall; plants such as cycas, Dieffenbachia, hydrangeas and palms flourish in a sheltered light well.

Below, left *Choisya ternata* 'Sundance', *Buxus sempervirens* trimmed into a globe shape and *Osmanthus heterophyllus* liven up the view from a basement flat.

Below, right *Cymbalaria muralis* is draped over a bold frame hung on brickwork, to produce a striking contrast in pattern and texture that brightens this dingy light well.

(*Polystichum setiferum*) and hostas. Ivy may seem an uninspired choice, but it is an incredibly useful plant that will grow anywhere and look good all year. Some variegated types, such as *Hedera canariensis* 'Gloire de Morengo', will retain their creamy markings in shade, but may only be hardy to 0°C/32°F. *H. helix* 'Angularis Aurea' is a tougher plant that will survive anywhere, with leaves that yellow as they age. All ivies do well in shade, but not all will retain their colour; *H. helix* 'Buttercup' is yellow in sunshine but pale green in shade.

A suitable plant can transform any spot, so don't give up on the dark corners. *Fatsia japonica* has spectacular leaves and flowers in autumn. Mahonia bears sweet-smelling flowers (*M. aquifolium* has leaves that turn red-purple in winter and the larger *M.* x *media* 'Charity' has bright yellow flowers from late autumn right through winter). You can use perennials and annuals to give seasonal colour. Hellebores (*Helleborus niger,* Christmas rose, and *H.* x *hybridus,* Lenten rose) flower in winter, followed by omphalodes (*O. cappadocica* has bright blue flowers). Pulmonaria will provide interest in spring (*P.* 'Lewis Palmer' has white-spotted leaves and flowers that turn from pink to blue as they open; *P. rubra* has bright green leaves and salmon-red flowers). Bleeding heart (*Dicentra spectabilis*) and deadnettle (*Lamium maculatum*) follow in early summer. Tobacco plants and busy Lizzies will flower throughout the summer and into autumn, overlapping with Japanese anemones (*A. hupehensis* and

A. x *hybrida*), which will give colour until the first hard frosts. This is only a selection, but it does show how easy it is to use perennials and annuals to achieve all-year colour in even the darkest sites.

Although suffering from lack of sunlight, there are advantages to the environment often found in a light well or basement: the sheltered aspect will protect more tender plants and the shade will delay the soil drying out. The soil will need watering if the surrounding walls cause a rain shadow, but once there the water should provide maximum benefit as it will not evaporate. (More ideas for gardening in dark areas are given in 'Shady plots', page 60). Unpromising as it may seem, your dark, dank light well or basement area can be transformed into an attractive little garden.

More than any other type of garden space, a balcony is a direct extension of your house, so if you are designing one it's worth bearing in mind the style of your interior decoration. This is not to say that you should be restricted to using exactly the same colours and styles, but a balcony off a minimalist room, for example, runs the risk of looking out of place if it is decorated with a riot of colours, and a few well-chosen sculptural plants such as agave, hostas and phormium would probably work better.

Before you start using a balcony you must ensure it is strong and safe for your purpose. This is particularly important in older buildings, where a balcony may look much more sturdy than it actually is. At this stage it needs to be treated in the same way as a roof and inspected by a professional who can assess its safety and load-bearing capacity. You also need to check that drainage is adequate, and that excess water from the containers will not cascade on to balconies below.

The two main factors influencing your choice of plants will be the amount of sun and wind the balcony receives. There is little you can do if the site is very shady, apart from choose plants that thrive in shade (see page 63). If it is windy, you may need to provide shelter. Sturdy trellis fixed to the railings will give good protection and can be used as a support for climbers. Deciduous climbers are often a sensible choice as they offer less resistance to the stronger winter winds and most deciduous plants are tougher than evergreens. If you do want year-round greenery, ivy is a good choice as it is resilient and does not take up too much space. More delicate specimens can be planted in the shelter of the trellis, to give seasonal interest. Work out exactly where the prevailing wind comes from and plant accordingly, using plants such as elaeagnus, escallonias, hebes and fuchsias, or any of the plants listed in 'Plants for exposed situations' (page 59) in the least sheltered areas.

Where you position the containers will depend on the shape of the balcony, but it is usually a good idea to put large containers at the ends where the structure is probably strongest and where they will not block access. Rectangular troughs are the most economical in terms of space as they can be fitted snugly against the railings. You can put the bulk of the planting into troughs at either end, adding interest with a few well-placed ornamental pots. Large containers on a balcony are usually best in plastic, which is light and retains water well. If necessary, smaller pots in more attractive materials can be positioned so as to hide the plastic. You can buy special metal brackets to keep containers firmly fixed in place; remember a balcony at any height will be particularly exposed to wind – and gales can be strong enough to lift trees that are firmly rooted in the ground.

Containers can also be attached to the balcony's railings. You can hang them on the outside, or on the inside, or both, but always make absolutely sure

The airy environment of a balcony offers many creative possibilities. Glass walls bring surrounding trees into the space. A single agave or even a sculpture can provide a striking alternative to cascading flowers. And when a whole community works together, traditional window boxes can create an amazing effect.

BALCONIES

Left A balcony jungle of cordyline, bamboo and tree ferns (*Dicksonia antarctica*).

Below, left Exuberant pelargoniums and *Nerium oleander* tumble over the edges of a minute balcony.

Below, right Driftwood and wind-tolerant plants such as helichrysum provide a foreground counterpoint to the spectacular riverside view.

they are well secured. Trailing plants such as ivy, trailing lobelia (*L. erinus*), nasturtiums and *Helichrysum petiolare* will all look attractive from both inside the balcony and below. You can use tough low-growing plants, such as pelargoniums, double busy Lizzies or heathers, to give clumps of colour along the tops of the troughs. Avoid plants that grow too tall as they will be buffeted by the wind and also tend to grow outwards, towards the light and away from you.

If you are working with a very confined space like a balcony, it is important to make the most of the verticals. You can train climbers up the back wall on trellis, and use pots and half baskets for temporary displays. Extending trellis overhead to form an arbour is another idea, and if you want a more solid shade it is worth considering a retractable awning. These are more stable than umbrellas and fit more neatly into the rectangular shape of a balcony.

ROOFS

Left Pile it high: climbers, a balcony and a roof terrace make use of every level of this house's exterior.

A roof garden can consist of anything from a small strip outside a window to an entire terrace where you can grow large plants and sit out. Whatever the size of the space, you must check that the roof is strong enough to meet your demands before you start gardening. A thorough structural survey by a professional should give you the load-bearing capacity of the site. It is important that the survey explains this in detail, as the amount of weight a roof can support may vary considerably over the area as a whole and you will need the information to position containers and furniture safely. A survey this detailed may seem expensive but will prevent the potentially far greater cost of repairs at a later date.

The boundaries of a roof space need to perform three functions: providing safety, creating shelter and maximizing or minimizing the view. For safety, there should be a barrier to at least waist height that is solid enough to prevent anyone falling off the roof. Railings, toughened glass or a brick wall are possible options. For shelter, you will need to erect some sort of windbreak above the solid barrier. Shelter is even more important than the amount of sunshine the space receives as, depending on the height of the roof and the surrounding buildings, the wind speed can reach double that at ground level. The range of plants you can grow will be severely restricted in an exposed site.

Work out which way the prevailing wind comes from and create a filter that will slow the wind and reduce its force. If you put up a solid screen the wind will simply go over or round it with increased strength. Trellis, hedging or groups of shrubs all act as good windbreaks, and will also provide shade if the midday sun is too hot. It is best to position tough plants (see 'Plants for exposed situations', page 59) around the edge of the roof and grow more delicate specimens in the sheltered area within. Trellis takes up less room than hedging or shrubs, and can be used to support plants, but must be strong enough to withstand the wind. Batons 2 x 3cm/^{3}/$_4$ x 1^1/$_4$ in treated with preservative are usually sufficient. Pierced walls, slatted timber or wattle fencing will all do just as well, depending on the degree of cover you want.

The boundary of the roof should also maximize a good view, or block out an unsightly one, or provide privacy if the space is overlooked. Tall trellis or shrubs can be used to hide unsightly buildings that spoil the outlook; tough but attractive evergreens such as Mexican orange blossom (*Choisya*), escallonia or mahonia are perfect for the job.

The surface of the roof may need treating before you can use it. Asphalt is not tough enough to withstand daily wear and tear. Lightweight paving slabs, gravel, bark, decking or even artificial turf are all relatively light and suitable for roofs. As at ground level, flooring can be used to create an illusion of greater depth or width. Wooden planks will always draw the eye along their length, and emphasize whatever direction they are laid in. Square areas can be made to appear larger and more interesting if you lay paving diagonally rather than straight across.

Conversely, a circular or square pattern will make an area appear more enclosed.

Access to water and adequate drainage are very important in a roof garden. It is really worth having an outdoor water supply installed and, unless you are very conscientious, it is also a good idea to consider an irrigation system as soil will dry out incredibly quickly. The sun will beat down, the wind will dry the plants and the containers are unlikely to be deep enough to allow the soil to store much moisture. Some plants will thrive in these conditions. Those with small or grey leaves such as lavender, rosemary and potentilla lose less water through evaporation, as do plants with hairy leaves like rabbit's ears (*Stachys byzantina*) and hairy canary clover (*Lotus hirsutus*). Sedums and euphorbias have thick, fleshy leaves that conserve water and help the plant survive in a harsh environment (see page 59 for more suggestions). Even these plants, however, will need a regular supply of water, especially during the summer months. Set the irrigation so it gives the necessary minimum and then top up by hand as required.

Below Walls provide a sheltered environment for fuchsias, tobacco plants, roses, clematis and lavender.

Containers and raised beds are the two planting options. Raised beds will support larger plants and will not dry out so fast, but are significantly heavier than containers. Your survey will tell you if it is safe to place raised beds in areas that have some structural support, such as at the edge of the roof. The walls and base of the bed can be constructed from treated timber, metal or plastic. Leave a 5cm/2in gap between the base of the bed and the roof and insert drainage holes at 15cm/6in intervals in the base. There should also be a 5–10cm/2–4in layer of gravel, measuring about a quarter of the total depth. On top of this put down a semi-permeable layer of geo-textile that will allow water through but not roots. Any that do work their way through will eventually reach the gap between the bed and the roof and go no further.

Containers are more flexible in terms of size and positioning, but remember that even the lightest plastic pot will weigh a considerable amount when filled with damp soil and a large plant. Containers should be as large as possible, securely fixed in place with wire or metal brackets and raised slightly off the ground with terracotta feet or bricks. This will ensure good drainage and allow you to see if the roots are growing through the bottom of the pot. When choosing the container, bear in mind that nonporous substances such as plastic, fibreglass and metal will dry out more slowly than terracotta. Placing crocks at the bottom of the pot to ensure good drainage and a thick mulch on top to prevent evaporation will enable the container to retain water without becoming soggy (see page 99 for more on care of containers).

Compost usually weighs less than top soil and can be lightened further by mixing with perlite or vermiculite. Unfortunately this will also cause the compost to dry out faster. Rockwool, often used by professional designers, is lightweight and only needs a layer 10cm/4in deep to support most plants. It sits on a drainage layer, but has no nutritional value so you have to feed the plants and provide mulch to prevent evaporation. Rockwool is not particularly easy to obtain and in most cases using mixed compost is an easier option.

With care almost any plant can be grown in a container on a roof. Use the wind-tolerant plants on page 59 to provide shelter and the drought-tolerant plants on the same page to fill the gaps. You can then give the more delicate plants the best positions. Bear in mind, however, that the temperature of a sunny roof may drop considerably at night.

You will almost certainly need some form of shade, and trellis, fixed awnings or umbrellas are all possible choices, depending on the degree of shade required. You may also want to install artificial lighting to emphasize a particular plant or area (see page 115 for lighting suggestions). As with all gardens, consider the time of day you will be out there and what you will be doing, and plan accordingly.

STEPS

E ven if your only outdoor area is a flight of stairs leading to your front door, there is still scope for a garden. You can either grow plants on the steps themselves or train them over the wall. The main function of stairs is access, so you'll have to leave enough room for them to be safely used and choose plants that will not spread out.

Wide steps can accommodate a row of pots on each level. Square containers may be the most suitable for this situation as they will fit snugly into the corner and contain the maximum amount of soil. Colourful annuals are a good choice for small pots in summer, and the season can be extended using winter pansies (*Viola* cultivars) or small heathers and skimmias, which will not outgrow the containers too fast. Always fix the pots in place securely using garden wire.

If you have open metalwork stairs you may be able to grow a climber in a large container underneath them. Many climbers, particularly clematis and honeysuckle, like to have their roots in shade and will happily scramble up steps. Wires fixed below the handrail will allow the plants to decorate the steps without blocking the way. Even if the steps are in deep shade, ivy or winter jasmine (*Jasminum nudiflorum*) could be grown in this manner. Space permitting, you could grow a climber in a large container at the top of the stairs and allow it to trail downwards. Climbers with woody stems, such as wisteria, Chilean potato vine (*Solanum crispum*) and

Left A simple arrangement of lights draws the visitor down the steps and into the garden.

Below *Sutera cordata* plants and a red pelargonium elegantly adorn this staircase.

climbing hydrangea (*H. anomala* subsp. *petiolaris*), are probably too bulky to use on stairs, but thinner plants, such as clematis, chocolate vine (*Akebia quinata*) or summer jasmine (*Jasminum officinale, J. x stephanense*), would be perfect for a sunny spot.

If you have spiral stairs, you could fix small pots at the narrow end of the steps or train plants up the centre using wires as a framework. You could also attach containers to the wall, as long as they don't obstruct access, or train up climbers on wire or trellis. Before choosing plants to grow against a wall check which way it faces, as this will affect the amount of sun received (see page 71).

A simple scheme of only one or two colours can sometimes be the most effective choice for a series of containers. A range of blues and whites, for example, can create much more of an impact than a riot of every colour available. A graduation of colours can also be very effective, changing from dark to light as you climb the stairs. Whatever you choose, make your planting lush, cramming as much as you can into the space you have. (For more on growing plants in containers, see 'Containers', page 94.)

EXPOSED
PLACES

Left In this rooftop garden tall phormiums and *Arundo donax* are cleverly placed to break the force of the wind and ensure privacy, while the rough wooden boards edging the raised bed provide welcome warmth to contrast with the concrete of the floor and the balustrade.

Below Dogwood (*Cornus alba* 'Sibirica') and euonymus (*E. fortunei*) also make good windbreaks.

Even if your garden is in an urban environment, it is not necessarily protected from the elements. Buildings tend to channel wind, increasing it greatly in speed and strength. Roof gardens and balconies are particularly exposed to both sun and wind, which can create drought conditions for the plants.

Wind can be one of the most harmful factors affecting a garden plant: as well as drying the surface of the plant it damages leaves and stems and causes stunted or lopsided growth. Too much sun can scorch new growth and cause excess evaporation. Plants with large, thin leaves, such as ferns, dead nettle (*Lamium maculatum*) and Himalayan blue poppy (*Meconopsis betonicifolia*), are particularly at risk from water loss. Plants with narrow leaves, such as rosemary and lavender, or those with a downy covering, such as rabbit's ears (*Stachys byzantina*), are much better adapted to conserve water.

Luckily, unlike with shade and soil problems, the effects of exposure can be moderated or even prevented fairly easily. Wind cannot be stopped, but it can be filtered or deflected. Filtering through trellis, openwork screens or wind-tolerant plants is the best option, as these permeable barriers will slow down the wind to a level where it is no longer harmful. In order to be effective a barrier needs to be about 3m/10ft high and the batons of trellis at least 2 x 3cm/³⁄₄ x 1¹⁄₄in.

Always protect vulnerable young plants from wind by supporting them with stakes that can be removed when the plants are 1–2 years old and firmly rooted in the soil. Prune shrubs gently in autumn to stop them blowing about too much. Roses and buddleja in particular benefit from being part-pruned in autumn and then cut to the correct size in spring. Climbers should be firmly tied in so their roots remain well anchored in the soil. Summer winds usually cause less structural damage than those at other times of year, but can dry a plant faster than the sun. Reduce water loss by covering the soil with a heavy mulch of well-rotted manure, mushroom compost or bark.

All the plants listed on the next page can be used in exposed situations, either as specimens or as protection for more tender plants.

Below Here a backing of trellis offers some wind protection
a mixed planting that includes red *Dahlia* 'Bishop of Llandaff
(top left), purple *Verbena bonariensis* rising at the back and t
lustrous-leaved *Pittosporum tobira* (front right).

Below *Salvia officinalis* (*top*) and *Yucca gloriosa* (*bottom*) both tolerate drought.

LANTS FOR EXPOSED SITUATIONS

WIND-TOLERANT PLANTS

Trees & shrubs

cer (maple)

erberis (barberry)

uxus sempervirens (box)

hoisya (Mexican orange blossom)

ornus (dogwood)

rataegus (hawthorn)

ytisus (broom)

uchsia

enista (broom)

ebe

edera (ivy)

ex aquifolium (holly)

iburnum

Perennials

rundo donax

entaurea (cornflower)

entranthus ruber (red valerian)

uonymus

eranium (cranesbill)

athyrus latifolius (perennial pea)

hormium

otentilla

Annuals & bulbs

ny which are low growing

rocus

ranthis (winter aconite)

arcissus – dwarf

DROUGHT-TOLERANT PLANTS

Shrubs

Buddleja

Buxus sempervirens (box)

Caryopteris (blue spiraea)

Cistus (rock rose)

Ficus (fig)

Hebe

Lavandula (lavender)

Philadelphus (mock orange)

Rosmarinus (rosemary)

Yucca

Perennial & annuals

Agapanthus (African blue lily)

Agave

Alchemilla mollis

Armeria (thrift)

Dianthus (pink)

Eryngium (sea holly)

Erysimum cheiri (wallflower)

Eschscholzia californica
   (California poppy)

Geranium (cranesbill)

Oenothera biennis (evening primrose)

Papaver orientale (oriental poppy)

Pennisetum (fountain grass)

Penstemon

Salvia officinalis (common sage)

Stachys byzantina (rabbit's ears)

The range of plants you can grow in a shady garden will be affected by the dampness or dryness of the soil and the density of the shade. Ground beneath trees and at the base of north- and east-facing walls will be very dry, but other shady areas may be very moist, as the sun will not dry the soil. Some soil under trees may receive dappled sunlight and areas shaded in winter may be sunny for part of the day in summer, when the sun is higher.

Soil in dry shade should be prepared with organic material before planting and mulched at least once a year. Water new seedlings well. A raised bed 30cm/12in high and 60cm/24in from a tree can greatly expand your planting because, although the area will still be shady, the soil in the bed will provide nutrients that would otherwise have been leached away by the tree. Box, ivy, euphorbias, dead nettles (*Lamium maculatum*) and periwinkles will all survive in dry shade. Ferns, foxgloves, snowdrops, *Mahonia japonica* and hostas need moister soil to do well.

Many shade-loving plants have large, thin, dark leaves which are suited to making the most of low light levels. If your garden receives a little light you will be able to grow variegated plants that will, in turn, make the area seem lighter still. Many ivies – *Hedera helix* 'Adam' (pinky-white variegations), *H.h.* 'Glacier' (white), *H.h.* 'Oro di Bogliasco' (syn. *H.h.* 'Goldheart') (yellow) – periwinkle (*Vinca*) and euonymus will remain variegated in fairly low light levels. Pale-leaved plants can also lighten a dark area; for example, *Choisya*

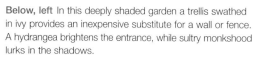

Below, left In this deeply shaded garden a trellis swathed in ivy provides an inexpensive substitute for a wall or fence. A hydrangea brightens the entrance, while sultry monkshood lurks in the shadows.

Below, right Purple hostas, dome-headed white hydrangeas and white lilies flourish in a shady back garden.

ternata 'Sundance', golden creeping Jenny (*Lysimachia nummularia* 'Aurea'), tobacco plants (*Nicotiana* 'Lime Green') and monkey flower (*Mimulus luteus*). Most variegated plants do best in dappled shade and some may revert to a single colour in very dark conditions.

One or two planting schemes will simply not work in deep shade and are best avoided. Silver- and blue-leaved plants need sun, as do lawns, which will become patchy and mossy in shade. The only herbs that do well in shade are parsley, chives and mint.

Clockwise from top right Plants for shady gardens: *Helleborus foetidus*; Solomon's seal (*Polygonatum*); ferns such as lady fern (*Athyrium filix-femina*).

Below The variegated leaves of plants such as *Hosta crispula* – seen here in front of *Darmera peltata*, with the yellow spires of *Ligularia przewalskii* rising above – will liven up a gloomy space.

EEP SHADE

ees & shrubs
onifers
orsythia suspensa
chsia
edera (ivy)
drangea
rria japonica 'Pleniflora'
eris
ses – some
nca (periwinkle)

erennials & biennials
onitum
quilegia
strantia
rns
ranium (cranesbill)
elleborus
sta
panese anemone
lygonatum (Solomon's seal)

nuals & bulbs
anthis (winter aconite)
patiens (busy Lizzie)
ies – some
naria annua (honesty)
yosotis (forget-me-not)
cotiana (tobacco plant)
imula
la

VARIEGATED/ BRIGHT FOLIAGE

Look out for the following Latin names:
aureus, golden; *albopictus,* painted white; *aureomarginata,* golden edged; *maculatus,* spotted; *marginata,* edged; *punctatus,* dotted; *variegata,* variegated.

Aucuba japonica 'Crotonifolia' (spotted laurel)
Berberis thunbergii 'Rose Glow'
Carex oshimensis 'Evergold' (sedge)
Choisya ternata 'Sundance' (Mexican orange blossom)
Elaeagnus x *ebbingei* 'Gilt Edge'
Euonymus fortunei 'Silver Queen' (spindle)
Hebe x *franciscana* 'Variegata'
Hosta (many variegated)
Ilex aquifolium 'Silver Queen' (holly)
Ligustrum ovalifolium 'Auruem' (golden privet)
Pachysandra terminalis 'Variegata'
Phormium tenax 'Dazzler' (New Zealand flax)
Vinca minor 'Variegata' (periwinkle)

OVERLOOK

Above, left An intimate arbour created with an overhead vine and raspberry canes.

Above, right And one screened by bamboo, sweet Cicely (*Myrrhis*), laburnum, goatsbeard (*Aruncus dioicus*) and Solomon's seal (*Polygonatum*).

SHRUBS TO SCRAMBLE OVER SUPPORT

Sun	Sun/light shade	Any position
Ceanothus arboreus 'Trewithen Blue' (Californian lilac)	*Actinidia kolomikta*	*Hedera* (ivy)
C. 'Autumnal Blue'	*Akebia quinata* (chocolate vine)	*Hydrangea anomala* subsp. *petiolaris* (climbing hydrangea)
Clematis cirrhosa	*Clematis alpina*	*Parthenocissus quinquefolia* (Virginia creeper)
C. montana	*C. armandii*	
Jasminum officinale (summer jasmine)	*C. macropetala*	
J. x *stephanense*	*Lonicera henryi* (honeysuckle)	
Vitis 'Brant' (grape vine)	*L. japonica*	
	L. periclymenum (woodbine)	
	L. tragophylla	
	Vitis coignetiae (ornamental vine)	
	Wisteria	

A garden is ideally secluded, but if you are trying to create a tiny garden in a town or city you will probably find that your space is overlooked by neighbouring buildings. There are two main strategies that you can use to minimize an unattractive or dominating object: put up a screen to hide it or create a focal point to draw the eye away.

Taking up as much as 90cm/36in even when clipped, a hedge will almost certainly be too bulky a barrier for a very restricted area, unless it is the main feature of a front garden. In this case choose slow-growing plants such as yew or box and keep them trimmed. Privet and shrubby honeysuckle (*Lonicera nitida*) grow faster, but will take up much more space.

Brick walls and solid fences give the greatest sense of privacy, but can make a small garden seem very enclosed and even oppressive. Your best option may be to fix trellis on top of a 1.2–1.5m/4–5ft wall or fence, and train climbers along it. This will provide a less claustrophobic screen than a completely solid boundary and will not take up as much room as a hedge or large shrubs (a fence and climber can be kept as narrow as 20cm/8in).

Solid shrubs and climbers such as viburnum, escallonia and ivy provide an attractive screen without taking up too much room. *Viburnum tinus* is a compact evergreen shrub that will give you small flowers throughout late winter and spring and dark blue-black fruits after that. *V.t.* 'Eve Price' grows to a maximum 3m/10ft and has pink buds opening into creamy-white flowers. *V.t.* 'Gwenllian' has darker pink buds and is slightly smaller.

Training plants over the top of your garden will also create a sense of privacy. Depending on the level of cover you want, you can use either wooden beams or wires as supports. An illusion of a solid screen is better than the real thing, which would block out light and air. Some plants need sturdier supports than others: wisteria and climbing hydrangea (*H. anomala* subsp. *petiolaris*) require strong wooden beams, while ivy, clematis or jasmine (*Jasminum officinale, J.* x *stephanense*) could rest on wires. Leave 1.2m/4ft between rows to give sufficient cover without blocking out too much light, and prune well; you want leafy young shoots, not solid woody stems. On a smaller scale, you could create an arbour by training climbers over either trellis or a wire arch and positioning a seat inside.

Tall plants in troughs can give privacy to a window. You can create a screen using plants such as foxgloves, Japanese anemones (*A. hupehensis, A.* x *hybrida*) or bear's breeches (*Acanthus spinosus*). Alternatively, fix wires over the window and train climbers such as morning glory, nasturtiums or perennial peas (*Lathyrus latifolius*) along them.

The shrubs listed in the box above will all trail along overhead supports. A wider selection of climbers is given on page 72. Bear in mind that some climbers mix well with others (ivy, clematis and roses), while others work better as a single specimen (wisteria, climbing hydrangea).

POLLUTED

Even a tiny garden can help to mitigate the effects of atmospheric and noise pollution common in towns and cities today. The leaves of trees and shrubs filter pollution and dust and improve air quality by absorbing carbon dioxide and producing oxygen. Just one small tree, such as hawthorn (*Crataegus laevigata* 'Paul's Scarlet') or holly, will benefit the atmosphere of your garden considerably. To a certain extent, foliage can also block out unwanted noises and create an illusion of quiet. Alternative sounds within the garden, such as water moving or wind rustling through grasses, will also help.

As a general rule plants that are naturally vigorous and easy to grow will not be affected much by pollution, which is why buddleja so often appears on building sites and along railway lines. Plants with glossy, leathery or tough leaves, such as holly or camellia, also often thrive in adverse conditions as the pollution in the air cannot penetrate the plant.

Fortunately, most plants will survive in a polluted atmosphere if they are given suitable conditions such as good soil and the correct amount of shelter, but their growth may be restricted and they may suffer from excessive leaf loss in autumn. Always enrich the soil with organic matter before planting in a polluted environment.

If you live on a particularly busy road consider the pollution-tolerant trees or shrubs listed in the box opposite, either as specimen plants or as a screen against noise and fumes.

SITES

Left and below, clockwise from left Plants for polluted sites: hydrangea, honeysuckle (*Lonicera periclymenum*) and magnolia (*M. wilsonii*).

PLANTS FOR POLLUTED SITES

Trees

Acer (maple)
Cercis siliquastrum (Judas tree)
Ilex (holly)
Magnolia
Malus (crab apple)
Prunus
Pyrus (ornamental pear)
Taxus baccata (yew)

Shrubs

Berberis
Buddleja
Camellia
Campsis radicans (trumpet vine)
Ceratostigma
Clematis – most
Cytisus (broom)
Escallonia
Forsythia
Hebe
Hibiscus
Hydrangea
Lonicera (honeysuckle)
Pyracantha (firethorn)
Roses – most
Rosmarinus officinalis (rosemary)
Sarcococca (Christmas box)
Skimmia
Syringa vulgaris (lilac)
Viburnum

WALLS

t is important to know which way a wall faces as the direction will control the amount of sun and rain a plant receives (always remember that a south-facing wall or fence is actually on the *north* side of the garden!). The greatest shade will be at the base of a wall, fence or hedge facing north, followed by one facing east. Woodland plants such as ivy, honeysuckle and all ferns will do well here. To get the full benefit of a sunny wall, on the other hand, it needs to be sheltered. A south-facing wall in a warm courtyard will support morning glory, *Actinidia kolomikta* and passion flower, while a wall facing the same way on a rooftop will be too exposed for the same plants to thrive.

There is a common misconception that you can grow anything against a south-facing wall and almost nothing against a north-facing one. In fact, there is a range of plants particularly suited to each aspect.

North-facing walls These beds are shady and tend to be dry. Many plants that would ideally prefer a sunny aspect will do perfectly well here; for example, winter jasmine (*Jasminum nudiflorum*), Virginia creeper (*Parthenocissus quinquefolia*) and some roses. The only fruit tree that will thrive in this position is the morello cherry (*Prunus cerasus*). Many plants listed on page 72 as suitable for north-facing sites have white or pale flowers that show up in low light.

South-facing walls Often considered the easiest to grow plants against, south-facing walls can be very hot and dry. Anything with Mediterranean origins will thrive here. Herbs, grey-leaved plants, annuals and most perennials will enjoy the heat and do well as long as you give them sufficient water. The plants will be sheltered from cold winds by the wall, but they will dry out very quickly in the sun. Add plenty of compost when planting and mulch thickly to conserve moisture. Brightly coloured flowers look especially good in the strong light.

East-facing walls Receiving no afternoon sun, an east-facing wall is prone to frost, which can be harmful to early-flowering plants. The bright morning sun of an east-facing site can also damage plants by melting frost rapidly, causing an abrupt rise in temperature that shocks the plant. The delicate buds of plants such as camellia and fruit trees put them particularly at risk, while flowering quince and forsythia, which flower just as early but have hardier buds, are better suited to these conditions. The amount of sunshine an east-facing bed receives may vary considerably with the seasons, as the sun rises higher in the sky during summer.

West-facing walls In many ways this is the ideal aspect. West-facing walls are kept warm by the afternoon sun and sheltered from cold winds, do not heat up too quickly in the morning and receive the most rainfall. Roses, clematis and fruit trees will grow particularly well in west-facing conditions, but almost any plant will survive.

Below A trellis clothed in ivy, with evergreens in columns and clipped balls completing the decorative effect.

Right Pelargoniums in wall-mounted pots provide a dazzling display of colour right through the summer.

PLANTS FOR WALLS

North-facing walls

Clematis – some

Cotoneaster

Ferns

Forsythia suspensa

Garrya elliptica (silk tassel bush)

Jasminum nudiflorum
  (winter jasmine)

Lonicera (honeysuckle) – some

Osmanthus delavayi

Parthenocissus henryana

P. quinquefolia (Virginia creeper)

Ribes (flowering currant)

Roses – some

Sarcococca (Christmas box)

South-facing walls

Abutilon

Campsis radicans (trumpet vine)

Ceanothus

Cistus (rock rose)

Eccremocarpus scaber
  (Chilean glory flower)

Fruit trees

Ipomoea (morning glory)

Jasminum officinale
  (summer jasmine)

Leptospermum (tea tree)

Nerine

Pelargonium

Roses – most

East-facing walls

Chaenomeles (flowering quince)

Clematis macropetala

Euonymus fortunei (spindle)

Forsythia

Humulus lupulus 'Aureus'
  (golden hop)

Hydrangea

Jasminum nudiflorum (winter
  jasmine)

Lathyrus latifolius (perennial pe

Lonicera (honeysuckle) – some

Prunus

Pyracantha

Roses – some

West-facing walls

Camellia

Chimonanthus praecox
  (wintersweet)

Choisya (Mexican orange
  blossom)

Clematis

Escallonia

Fruit trees

Jasminum (jasmine)

Magnolia

Roses – some

Solanum crispum (potato vine)

Wisteria

SEASONAL

Above, left Magnolias provide colour early in the year and then a strong backdrop for summer flowers.

Above, right In autumn most maples (*Acer*) turn wonderful shades of yellow, gold or red.

NTEREST

I n a tiny garden that may be no bigger than a single flowerbed or window box it is particularly important to choose a selection of plants that will provide colour and interest throughout the year. The shrubs listed in the box under 'Year-round interest', most of which are evergreen, will give you colour all year round but none are particularly striking. If you have room, these shrubs are useful as a backdrop for changing displays of the plants listed by season below. A single small pot with one bright plant will liven up a dark corner, and such containers can easily be moved around as the plants fade.

Spring interest Bulbs provide the earliest colour, and are useful in a small garden as you can fit them in at the base of a tree or shrub or among other plants in containers. Snowdrops, miniature daffodils, crocus and wood anemones (*A. blanda*) are all good.

Any annuals planted out must be hardy, and most will not start looking good until summer. Biennials planted the previous autumn, such as foxgloves and wallflowers (*Erysimum cheiri* syn. *Cheiranthus cheiri*), will appear in mid-spring. If you forgot to plant them in the autumn you can buy more mature plants in early spring.

Most perennials concentrate on growing during this season, but bleeding heart (*Dicentra spectabilis*), aquilegias and aubrieta all flower early. In early spring many shrubs have flowers on bare stems. Forsythia, flowering quince, *Kerria japonica* and magnolia all bear attractive flowers before their leaves appear.

PLANTS FOR SEASONAL INTEREST

YEAR-ROUND INTEREST

Trees & shrubs
Berberis
Buxus sempervirens (box)
Calluna vulgaris (heather)
Choisya (Mexican orange blossom)
Escallonia
Hebe
Ilex (holly)
Mahonia
Pieris
Pyracantha
Viburnum tinus
Vinca

Perennials
Festuca glauca (blue fescue)
Phormium tenax (New Zealand flax)
Polypodium (fern)
Polystichum (fern)

SPRING INTEREST

Trees
Cercis siliquastrum (Judas tree)
Crataegus (hawthorn)
Magnolia stellata
Malus (crab apple)

Shrubs
Ceanothus
Chaenomeles (flowering quince)
Genista (broom)
Kerria japonica 'Pleniflora' (Jew's mantle)
Philadelphus (mock orange)
Pieris
Syringa (lilac)
Weigela
Wisteria

Perennials & biennials
Aquilegia
Dicentra spectabilis (bleeding heart)
Digitalis (foxglove)
Erysimum cheiri (wallflower)
Hesperis matronalis (sweet rocket)
Lunaria annua (honesty)
Myosotis (forget-me-not)
Omphalodes cappadocica
Pulmonaria

Bulbs
Allium
Crocus
Galanthus (snowdrop)

Hyacinthoides (bluebell)
Narcissus (daffodil)
Scilla
Tulipa

SUMMER INTEREST

Shrubs
Buddleja davidii
Ceratostigma
Fuchsia
Hebe
Hydrangea
Jasminum officinale
Lavandula (lavender)
Lavatera (mallow)
Lonicera (honeysuckle)
Rosa

Perennials
Alcea rosea (hollyhock)
Anemone hupehensis
A. x hybrida (Japanese anemone)
Argyranthemum
Dianthus (pink)
Geranium (cranesbill)
Helianthemum (rock rose)
Monarda
Papaver (poppy)
Verbena

From far left Daffodils herald the beginning of spring; the flowers of rock roses last only a day but will appear all through summer; the autumn-flowering clematis 'Bill MacKenzie' has pretty yellow flowers followed by fluffy seedheads that last well into winter; the long grey-green catkins of *Garrya elliptica* are borne from midwinter to early spring.

nuals & bulbs

ium
smos bipinnatus
chscholzia californica
  (California poppy)
adioli
lianthus annuus (sunflower)
moea (morning glory)
thyrus odoratus
  (sweet pea)
ium
cotiana (tobacco plant)
gella damascena
  (love-in-a-mist)
paver (poppy)
opaeolum (nasturtium)

TUMN INTEREST

ees & shrubs

er (maple)
nelanchier
llicarpa bodinieri
  var. *giraldii*
eratostigma
ematis tangutica
viticella
rthenocissus quinquefolia
  (Virginia creeper)
racantha (firethorn)
is (vine)

Perennials & biennials

Aconitum (monkshood)
Anemone hupehensis
A. x *hybrida*
  (Japanese anemone)
Aster (Michaelmas daisy)
Gaura lindheimeri
Kniphofia
Oenothera biennis
  (evening primrose)
Salvia
Verbena bonariensis

Annuals & bulbs

Colchicum speciosum
  (autumn crocus)
Dahlia
Helianthus annuus
  (sunflower)
Ipomoea (morning glory)
Tropaeolum (nasturtium)

WINTER INTEREST

Trees & shrubs

Berberis wilsoniae
Callicarpa bodinieri var.
  giraldii
Chimonanthus praecox
  (wintersweet)
Cotoneaster horizontalis

Daphne
Garrya elliptica
Ilex aquifolium (holly)
Jasminum nudiflorum
Pyracantha
Sarcococca (Christmas box)
Skimmia japonica
Viburnum

Perennials

Bergenia cordifolia
  (elephant's ears)
Brunnera macrophylla
Carex (sedge)
Helleborus (hellebore)
Iris unguicularis
Pulmonaria

Annuals & bulbs

Colchicum speciosum
  (autumn crocus)
Crocus sieberi
Cyclamen hederifolium
Eranthis (winter aconite)
Galanthus (snowdrop)
Leucojum vernum
  (spring snowflake)
Narcissus (daffodil)
Scilla
Viola x *wittrockiana* (pansy)

Summer interest This is the easy season; if anything there is too much choice. Most annuals complete their life cycles during summer and will flower repeatedly as long as you deadhead, water and feed them regularly. The bulbs of summer tend to be large and grand: alliums, lilies, crocosmia and gladioli give splashes of colour in early, mid- and late summer respectively. Plan your perennials so you have a selection flowering throughout the season; it is easy to end up with lots of flowers in early summer followed by dismal gaps as they die down.

The stars of the summer shrubs are roses. There is a rose for almost every situation and, according to your wishes, fragrance, repeat flowering and a huge range of colours are available.

Autumn interest This can be a mild season and many plants will carry on flowering until the first frosts or even beyond. The annuals busy Lizzies, tobacco plants, cosmos and pansies (*Viola* x *wittrockiana*) will continue to flower happily. Bulbs are best known for their appearance in spring, but crocus (*C. banaticus, C. cartwrightianus*) and autumn crocuses – *Colchicum speciosum* (pink), *C.s.* 'Album' (white) – flower now. Late perennials will lift the garden and monkshood, Japanese anemones (*A. hupehensis, A.* x *hybrida*), *Sedum spectabile* and *Verbena bonariensis* will all flower well into winter if your garden is sheltered.

Autumn is the time of bright berries and spectacular foliage, and it is here that shrubs come into their own. Virginia creeper (*Parthenocissus*

Below *Rosa* 'Climbing Iceberg' flowers profusely through summer and autumn.

Right The strong lines of topiary sustain this garden design through all the seasons.

quinquefolia), berberis and maples all have leaves that will turn varying shades of red, orange and purple. Other shrubs produce beautiful berries, many of which remain on the branches throughout winter. Cotoneaster berries are red, pyracantha yellow or orange and *Callicarpa bodinieri* var. *giraldii* the most amazing bright purple. Shrubs such as fuchsias, hydrangeas and roses will still be flowering in autumn.

Winter interest Having tidied the garden for winter all you need are a couple of focal points to see you through until spring. You can plant containers with evergreens and a single splash of seasonal colour in a small pot within the larger one; the small container can be moved as the colour fades. Heather, pansies (*Viola* x *wittrockiana*) and skimmia (*S. japonica*) are all useful seasonal fillers. Bulbs start appearing in mid-winter, and snowdrops and early crocus – *C. sieberi* subsp. *sublimis* 'Tricolor' (lilac, white and gold bands) – will give you pockets of colour right through to spring. As winter moves into spring the perennial Christmas and Lenten hellebores (*Helleborus niger, H. orientalis*) appear, followed by pulmonarias. Many shrubs flower at this time, but may look boring during the rest of the year. One good specimen is really all you need and daphne (*D. bholua* 'Jacqueline Postill'), viburnum (*V.* x *bodnantense* 'Dawn', *V. tinus* 'Gwenllian') or wintersweet (*Chimonanthus praecox*) would do perfectly. Remember that autumn colour, particularly berries, will remain on the branches of some plants for most of winter.

PLU

IDEAS

PRA

Plants for a tiny garden should be chosen carefully. Ideally each one should justify its place by having at least two good features. A long flowering season is an obvious attraction, but foliage, interesting bark, berries, scent, autumn colour and overall shape are all worth considering as well. It is also important to consider how big the plants will grow. Trees and shrubs can often be restricted by planting them in containers, trimming their roots or pruning regularly, but it is better to choose a plant that is roughly the right size and allow it to grow naturally. Hard pruning can be counter-productive as it frequently encourages new growth.

Small gardens are often sheltered environments where you may be able to grow exotic plants easily. Many of the large-leaved specimens, such as Tasmanian tree fern (*Dicksonia antarctica*), Chusan palm (*Trachycarpus fortunei*), *Agave americana* and *Cordyline australis*, are much tougher than they look and will give your garden a tropical feel. Mediterranean plants, such as rosemary, lavender, olive and in warmer areas even citrus trees – *C. limon* (lemon), *C. sinensis* (orange) – will thrive in a sunny and sheltered spot.

When selecting plants for a tiny garden it is usually best to choose your largest plants first and then experiment with smaller ones planted in between. Individual plants can be used as focal points, but having more than a couple that really stand out may only create a confused effect in a very restricted space. In a tiny garden you also need to think particularly carefully about whether the plants work well as a group. It is a good idea to introduce some contrasts as these will provide points of interest within the garden. Variations of foliage can be very effective, contrasting light and dark, feathery and leathery or even simply large and small.

Choose plant colours that work well together in the environment of your garden. Pastel colours come into their own in low-light levels and are particularly effective in a shady site. Brilliant reds and oranges are most striking in bright sunshine, and rich blues, purples and crimsons look lovely in the evening light. Bright, hot colours will draw the eye and you can use them as a focal point. Remember that green is a colour too; you can use shades of green to provide interest as well as a backdrop for other colours.

Trees You can have a tree in a very small garden, but you need to choose one that will not grow too large. Even within a genus the sizes can vary enormously: for example, *Acer pseudoplatanus* (sycamore) can reach 30m/100ft, while there are cultivars of *A. palmatum* that only grow to 10m/15ft.

If you have space for just one tree, try for at least two seasons of interest. Crab apples provide spring blossom, fruit and autumn colour, while amelanchiers (*A. canadensis, A.* x *grandiflora*) offer blossom, autumn colour and berries. Fruit trees will give you blossom and edible fruits and are usually grafted on to particular rootstocks so you know what

PLANTS
FOR A TINY
GARDEN

Above Tree ferns, grasses and bamboos make a miniature tropical forest in a small courtyard.

Right Chocolate vine (*Akebia quinata*) is a useful semi-evergreen climber that provides spicily scented flowers in early spring and fruit in summer.

their final size will be (see page 104 for more about fruit trees).

Weeping trees can look very attractive and come in compact varieties, such as Kilmarnock willow (*Salix caprea* 'Kilmarnock') or weeping purple birch (*Fagus sylvatica* 'Purpurea Pendula'). Within reason it is possible to limit the size of a tree by growing it in a container. Bay trees usually have a final height of 12m/40ft, but grown in a container they can be kept happily at 90cm/36in. If you do restrict a tree's growth in this way, you will need to give it extra care and attention to compensate for its unnatural environment. In particular, it will be at risk from drying out.

A selection of trees suitable for tiny gardens is listed on page 86. Those in the first list would work well as the main feature plant of a small garden. The second list contains miniature trees (mostly under 1.8m/6ft) that would fit almost anywhere, either in the ground or in a container, without dominating their surroundings.

Shrubs As with trees, choose a shrub with at least two features of interest; viburnum, for example, will provide colourful leaves, flowers and berries. Climbers, such as roses or clematis, can be trained through bushy shrubs to prolong the flowering season. Remember also that many climbers fulfil the same functions as bushy shrubs while taking up less room; honeysuckle and summer jasmine (*Jasminum officinale*), for example, will provide as effective a screen as the much more bulky escallonia.

Roses merit special consideration, since they come in a wide range of sizes and flower colours, which, as long as you choose carefully, can suit any situation. English roses, developed by David Austin, are particularly useful in a small garden as many combine the powerful scent of old roses with the ability to flower repeatedly throughout the summer. Patio (45cm/18in) and miniature roses (23–45cm/9–18in) are good in small spaces and most will do well in containers.

Perennials Perennials usually do better planted in beds rather than in containers. The extra soil will provide more support for their root systems and the extra space will allow you to stagger the flowering so that later species can take over as the earlier ones die back. Perennials are often tougher than annuals and plants can be found for all conditions; pinks, for example, will survive drought and *Alchemilla mollis* will thrive in both drought and deep shade. Feed your perennials in spring, deadhead, water and stake them as necessary and they will reward you with years of colour.

Many grasses are perennials and those that are annuals usually self seed freely so you get new plants each year. They range in size from squirrel tail grass (*Hordeum jubatum*), which grows to 50cm/20in, to bamboos over 20m/70ft high. Grasses are very invasive, but their size can be successfully curtailed by growing them in containers. Small bamboos that are suitable for a tiny garden include *Chusquea*

Below An orange tree will grow well in a pot and can be moved to a sheltered spot in winter if necessary.

TREES FOR A TINY GARDEN

Small trees

Acer japonicum (Japanese maple)

Amelanchier canadensis

Azara microphylla

Betula pendula 'Youngii' (Young's weeping birch)

Cercis siliquastrum (Judas tree)

Crataegus (hawthorn) – most

Fruit trees on dwarf rootstock

Juniperus scopulorum 'Skyrocket' (Rocky Mountain juniper)

Lagerstroemia indica (crepe flower)

Malus (crab apple) – most

Prunus (ornamental cherry) – most

Pyrus salicifolia 'Pendula' (weeping pear)

Taxus baccata 'Fastigiata' (yew)

Tiny trees

Acer palmatum (Japanese maple) – in a container

Citrus limon (lemon) – in a container

C. sinensis (orange) – in a container

Fagus sylvatica 'Purpurea Pendula' (weeping beech)

Ilex (holly) – most; in a container

Laurus nobilis (bay) – in a container

Magnolia stellata

Malus domestica (apple) – on M27 or very dwarf rootstock

Olea europaea (olive) – in a container

Picea glauca var. *albertiana* 'Conica'

Pittosporum tenuifolium

Salix caprea 'Kilmarnock' (Kilmarnock willow)

Taxus baccata 'Standishii' (yew)

eou (Chilean bamboo), *Phyllostachys nigra* (black mboo), *Pleioblastus viridistriatus* and *Semiarundinaria tuosa*; suitable grasses include *Briza maxima* (quaking ass), *Hordeum jubatum* (squirrel tail grass), *Miscanthus ensis* 'Kleine Fontäne' and *Molinia caerulea*.

nuals and biennials Annuals are very useful in a tiny rden for filling in gaps and providing colour throughout e summer. Most will keep on trying to produce seeds the following year and if you deadhead them before ey can set seed they will flower well into autumn and en winter. Many plants grown as annuals are actually ort-lived perennials, and if you live in a mild area apdragons and tobacco plants may flower for a cond year.

Annuals are divided into hardy plants, which can rvive frost, and half-hardy plants, which cannot. Hardy nuals, such as love-in-a-mist, sweet peas (*Lathyrus doratus*) and opium poppies (*Papaver somniferum*), n easily be grown from seed, either in trays or directly the soil where they are to flower. Half-hardy annuals e usually best grown under glass and if you want to ow them from seed it may be worth investing in a mini eenhouse. These take up very little room and can be attractive feature as well as a practical aid. Half-ardies are readily available to buy as small plants, but ant them out only once the risk of frost has passed and ot when your garden centre has an enticing display of em, which may be considerably earlier.

Annuals need more care than perennials as they do erything from germinating to setting seed in one year or

PLANTS FOR FRAGRANCE

Trees & shrubs

Aloysia triphylla (lemon verbena)

Azara microphylla

Cytisus battandieri (pineapple broom)

Hamamelis (witch hazel)

Lavandula (lavender)

Lonicera (honeysuckle) – many

Osmanthus

Philadelphus (mock orange)

Rosa (rose) – many

Sarcococca (Christmas box)

Syringa (lilac)

Perennials & biennials

Dianthus (pink)

D. barbatus (sweet William)

Erysimum cheiri (wallflower)

Herbs – most

Hesperis matronalis (sweet rocket)

Matthiola incana (stock)

Oenothera biennis (evening primrose)

Phlox paniculata

Annuals & bulbs

Cosmos atrosanguineus (chocolate cosmos)

Herbs – most

Hyacinthoides non-scripta (English bluebell)

Hyacinthus

Lathyrus odoratus (sweet pea)

Nicotiana (tobacco plant)

Reseda odorata (mignonette)

less. Most, apart from busy Lizzies and tobacco plants, require a certain amount of sunshine and all will need regular feeding and watering throughout the growing season.

Biennials grow over two years, developing roots and leaves in the first and flowers in the second. Many perennials, such as sweet William (*Dianthus barbatus*), provide a better display of colour if treated as biennials and replaced after the second year. Most biennials can be grown from seed, but in a restricted space you would probably do better to buy small plants in the autumn that will flower the following spring or summer. Wallflowers (*Erysimum cheiri*), hollyhocks (*Alcea rosea*) and forget-me-not (*Myosotis sylvatica*) are particularly attractive.

Bulbs Bulbs are extremely valuable in a tiny garden as they take up very little space, can grow under and around other plants and will provide colour early in the year, when little else is in flower. Bear in mind that plant heights can vary considerably, especially amongst daffodils and tulips. The hoop petticoat daffodil (*Narcissus bulbocodium*), for example, is only 10–15cm/4–6in tall, while *N.* 'Spellbinder' reaches 50cm/20in.

The group also includes corms (crocus, gladiolus and colchicum), tubers (dahlias and anemones) and rhizomes (some irises and lily-of-the-valley). These all have slightly different characteristics but grow in a similar way and usually need to be in the soil six months before they are to flower. Apart from

cyclamen, bulbs need some sunshine to thrive but most will do well planted around the base of shrubs. Only gladioli and crocosmia require full sun.

All bulbs take in nutrients via their leaves and it is important that you do not cut them down after flowering. You should remove the spent flowers but let the leaves remain for six to eight weeks so the bulb can replenish its reserves for the following year. This may look untidy, but cannot be avoided. What you can do instead is plant perennials and annuals so they grow up in front of the drooping leaves and hide them. Japanese anemones (*A. hupehensis, A.* x *hybrida*), cranesbill geraniums and aquilegias all make useful screens. Most bulbs can remain untouched in the soil and will come up year after year, and larger bulbs can be planted deeply (10cm/4in) to enable you to grow annuals over the top. The exceptions are gladioli and dahlias, which are not frost hardy and may need to be lifted in autumn, stored and replanted in spring.

Plants for fragrance In a tiny garden with room for only a handful of plants, fragrance is as important as colour. Many flowers are scented and some plants, such as rosemary, mint and thyme, have scented leaves. You can use a raised bed or a tall container to lift the plants above ground level, so that their fragrance may be more easily enjoyed. Scented plants also work wonderfully along a path or by a doorway where you will release their fragrance by brushing against them.

Cutting flowers However small your space, you can ensure a supply of flowers for the house by growing 'cut-and-come-again' varieties that produce more flowers to replace those you take. Sweet peas and repeat-flowering roses actually perform better if you remove their blooms, and annuals such as cosmos, snapdragons and dwarf sunflowers quickly reflower. Perennials like aquilegias, cornflowers, red valerian and scabious also quickly produce flowers again.

As long as you do not take all the blooms off the plants they will continue to flower, and you will be able to enjoy colour in the garden and in the house throughout the summer, possibly even longer.

Encouraging wildlife in your garden Although you won't have room to create a totally wild environment, you can attract birds and insects that will help you by eating pests such as slugs, snails and aphids. Provide cover and grow plants such as pyracantha, cotoneaster or berberis with berries that birds can eat in winter. As a very general rule, native plants are usually the most attractive to wildlife and single flowers rather than ornamental doubles or hybrids the most rich in nectar. Finally, don't use any pesticides or chemicals.

LAWNS & GROUND COVER

Left A lawn the size of a footstool makes a witty centrepiece for a little courtyard.

Below Another miniature lawn, this one with an edging of dwarf box (*Buxus sempervirens* 'Suffruticosa'), is an elegant variation on the theme.

The standard advice for a very small garden is that it is not worth having a lawn, as they require a lot of work and often don't do well. That said, a patch of grass, however tiny, can provide a much-needed oasis in an urban area. And although it is true that a tiny lawn will quickly suffer from wear and tear, if you are only dealing with a very limited area there is nothing to stop you simply digging up the grass and starting again.

To grow well, grass has two requirements that cannot be ignored: good, well-drained soil and a reasonable level of sunshine throughout the year. If you cannot provide both of these you should consider an alternative form of ground cover. Lawns also cannot survive too much traffic so if you regularly cross the grass you should put in stepping stones. Chairs and tables are better placed on a hard surface than on grass.

Making a lawn Prepare the site by removing old grass, stones and weeds and digging in compost, adding sand if the drainage is poor. Level the site using a rake. Then ideally leave for a month, to allow you to remove any weeds that grow up during this period. On a dry day, when the soil is not too damp, flatten the area by walking across it using tiny steps and wearing flat shoes. This will level the soil but not compact it. Then apply a granular fertilizer.

Turf is more convenient than seed as it looks good immediately, and for a tiny lawn it won't be prohibitively expensive. Turves should be laid within forty-eight hours of delivery, kept well watered and not walked on for four to six weeks. Water the area the night before laying the turf so the soil is moist but not waterlogged. Lay the turves in closely packed rows, staggering the rows so the joins do not form a grid. If you need to cut small strips to complete a row put them in the middle rather than at an end, to prevent them from drying out. Gaps that appear as the turf settles can be filled with a top dressing and seed. You can buy a ready-made dressing or make your own of three parts soil, six parts sand and one part organic compost.

Care of the lawn In a small garden a lawn will require as much or more care than a flowerbed. Cut the grass regularly from early spring to late autumn. Flat shears with long, right-angled handles may be more suitable than a mower for use in a restricted space.

Give the lawn a nitrogen-based feed in spring to encourage new growth and a general mix in autumn, and sweep away fallen leaves to prevent them forming a soggy covering. Raking the lawn with a spring-tined rake before you apply the feed in autumn will remove the thatch – the mixture of dead and living organic matter that accumulates at the base of the grass stems and prevents air, water and fertilizer reaching the soil. This process, called scarifying, may leave the grass looking worse than before, but the lawn will recover over the winter and in the long run its condition will be improved greatly.

If necessary you can aerate the lawn to improve drainage. Push a garden fork 5cm/2in into the soil and gently ease it back and forth, repeating at 15cm/6in intervals. Then sprinkle top dressing over the lawn (3kg per square metre/6lb per square yard) and brush into the holes. This will improve soil drainage, help the grass grow and discourage moss.

Alternatives to grass Other plants can be used to create an interesting patch, although none are particularly hard-wearing. Thyme and chamomile in particular give off a lovely fragrance when crushed. If you will be walking across the area regularly, lay paving stones and allow the plants to overlap the edges.

All the alternative lawns described below work best as a single type of plant. If you mix them you run the risk of cultivating what looks like a patch of weeds. Prepare the soil as for a traditional lawn and weed in between the plants until they are established. Small plants will settle in more quickly than larger specimens.

Chamomile Full sun and well-drained soil are vital. Once established it will prevent weeds growing and only need occasional trimming. *Chamaemelum nobile* 'Treneague' is very fragrant and gives good cover, but does not flower. *C.n.* 'Flore Pleno' has double, daisy-like flowers, but is less solid and better for edging.

Thyme This also needs full sun and well-drained soil. Culinary thyme (*Thymus vulgaris*) is too tall and bushy for a lawn; the prostrate species *T. polytrichus* or *T. serpyllum* are better. Both flower in summer, are fragrant and attract bees.

Moss The enemy of so many gardeners can be used as a lawn in shade. If you have a lot of moss simply pull up the grass and allow the moss to spread.

Clover Another traditional enemy. Clover needs full sun and well-drained soil, but can withstand drought. *Trifolium pratense* 'Susan Smith' will form a mat 15cm/6in deep, with pink flowers in early summer. *T. repens* 'Purpurascens Quadrifolium' is shorter, with maroon-centred leaves and small white flowers in summer. Both are semi-evergreen.

From left to right Heathers; *Sedum*; *Sempervivum*;
and ivy with *Lamium maculatum* 'Beacon Silver'.
All will provide useful ground cover for a small space.

ROUND COVER

un

meria (thrift)
ubrieta
eanothus prostrate species such as
  C. gloriosus
rica (heather)
rigeron karvinskianus
estuca glauca
eranium (cranesbill)
ypsophila repens
ebe pinguifolia 'Pagei'
elianthemum (rock rose)
uniperus horizontalis (creeping juniper)
  procumbens (prostrate juniper)
obularia maritima (sweet alyssum)
ysimachia nummularia (creeping Jenny)
osmarinus officinalis 'Prostratus'
  (prostrate rosemary)
antolina chamaecyparissus
  (cotton lavender)
aponaria ocymoides (tumbling Ted)
edum spathulifolium
empervivum tectorum (houseleek)
tachys byzantina (rabbit's ears)
anacetum
eucrium fruticans

un/part shade

ampanula carpatica
. cochleariifolia (fairies' thimbles)

C. portenschalgiana
C. poscharskyana
Persicaria affinis
Soleirolia soleirolii
  (mind your own business)

Shade

Ajuga reptans (bugle)
Arabis caucasica (rock cress)
Bergenia (elephant's ears)
Brunnera
Geranium macrorrhizum (cranesbill)
Hosta
Lamium maculatum (dead nettle)
Omphalodes cappadocica
Pachysandra terminalis
Pulmonaria
Saxifraga stolonifera 'Tricolor'
  (mother of thousands)
S. x urbium (London pride)
Tiarella cordifolia (foam flower)

Any position

Alchemilla mollis
Cotoneaster dammeri
Hedera (ivy)
Nemophila maculata (five spot)
N. menziesii (baby blue eyes)
Vinca minor (periwinkle)
Waldsteinia ternata

Gravel Gravel is a versatile ground cover, especially useful for brightening dark gardens, and you can position plants to create islands of colour. Before laying gravel, clear the ground of grass, weeds and any large stones and put down a sheet of semi-permeable geo-textile (bonded-fibre fleece or woven polypropylene are both suitable) that will allow water to drain away but prevent weeds pushing through. You can cut holes in the geo-textile layer to accomodate plants. Choose plants that form neat clumps and won't invade the gravel, such as thrift, blue fescue (*Festuca glauca*) and rock rose if the site is sunny or alchemilla and brunnera if it is shady. Also effective are drifts of small plants, such as *Iris pallida* 'Variegata' with its green- and white-striped leaves and blue flowers.

Ground-cover plants An interesting and easy way to cover a small area is to use ground-cover plants. Once established these plants need little maintenance and will prevent weeds growing, but many are invasive and can easily become weeds themselves. Create a path through the plants with stepping stones or gravel, enclosing gravel on either side with metal strips to stop it spreading.

If you want the space to be as appealing in winter as in summer choose evergreen plants to provide a covering throughout the year. Remember also to consider the final height of the plants. *Tanacetum* can reach 90cm/36in, while creeping Jenny (*Lysimachia nummularia*) will only grow to 5cm/2in.

The smaller your space the more important your containers are, enabling you to create a garden even if you have no flowerbed at all. Containers give you flexibility and allow you to alter the design as the seasons change and the plants grow. In a really tiny garden the choice of container is itself a central element of the design.

Almost anything will grow in a pot as long as there is enough room for the roots and you provide sufficient food and water, but some plants are more suitable for this treatment than others. Many trees and shrubs will not reach their full size in a container, but this will not necessarily do them any harm. However, you should aim to limit the size of a plant by no more than 10 per cent; plants will do best if you choose those that fit the space you have rather than trying to restrict them too much. As a rough guideline, containers should be at least one-quarter to one-third as tall as the intended final height of the plant and the same as the mature plant in diameter.

Most small trees and shrubs can be grown in containers and will give your pots a look of permanence (see page 86 for tree specimens recommended for tiny gardens). This method is very convenient if you want to grow plants such as oranges, lemons and olives, which have to be moved to a sheltered position during winter if grown in a cool climate.

Perennials often die down after flowering so the trick is to put them in a large container and grow a selection of plants that come up at different times. Grasses in particular make a spectacular permanent display that you can augment with bulbs and annuals. All annuals, biennials and bulbs will do well in pots. Pelargoniums actually flower better if their roots are restricted. Alpines are traditionally associated with shallow stone sinks, but will grow in any container as long as it is well drained.

Choosing containers You may find that a few larger containers give a more convincing illusion of space than a mass of tiny pots. One way of avoiding a fussy effect is to treat a group of containers as a single unit rather than a selection of individual items, linking them through material, colour, style or planting. Think vertically as well as horizontally and give your display height either by raising a container on a plinth (a pile of bricks is an easy way to do this) or by fixing pots to a fence or wall.

As well as looking more effective in a small space, bigger pots are easier to maintain, extend the range of plants you can grow and raise the plants up into your line of vision. A good minimum height and width to consider for permanent planting is 60cm/24in. All containers should have drainage holes and be frost resistant, unless you are prepared to move them indoors in winter.

The various materials available all have advantages and disadvantages. Real old stone is beautiful, but very heavy and often extremely expensive. Fake or reconstituted stone can look as

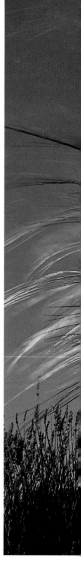

Below This dark courtyard is brightened by white walls, yellow doors and a profusion of flowers, including a mass of white petunias in an urn covered with stonecrop (*Sedum*).

Right *Dasylirion acrotrichum* underplanted with *Acaena* makes an impact in a terracotta planter.

od and cost a fraction of the price. The same applies
ead containers, and to fibreglass simulations of lead.
Terracotta comes in a wide range of glazed and
glazed colours. Unglazed pots will weather charmingly
n age, and you can speed up this process by painting
m with a solution of watered-down yoghurt. Unglazed
acotta is, however, nearly always slightly porous,
ch means that it is liable to dry out and is also at risk
n cracking caused by frost. To stop unglazed
acotta pots drying out too fast, line them with plastic
rce the plastic to make drainage holes) or spray a thin
er of polystyrene or insulating foam inside the pot.
ring periods of frost, move the pots to a sheltered
ot or wrap them in bubble wrap, horticultural fleece or
vspaper to prevent them freezing.

Plastic is cheap, light and does not dry out as fast as
acotta. It can be painted any colour and can always be
guised by trailing plants. Plastic does, however, become
tle with age and is not suitable for permanent planting
t will eventually crack and break.

Wooden troughs and boxes look wonderful but need
oe treated with preservative regularly. To avoid having
take out all the plants and soil every year, position a
stic container inside the wooden one. This will give
u the practical advantages of plastic with the
oearance of wood. Put the plastic trough in place
ore filling it as the compost will make it expand.

You do not need to limit yourself to custom-made
s. Anything that has drainage holes and can hold soil
d water can be used: watering cans, baskets, chimney
s and buckets all make good plant containers.

Below An arrangement of potted pink and white argyranthemums and purple verbena on wire staging takes up very little space and looks fresh and pretty.

Right Bamboos planted in big galvanized containers look dramatic and provide an efffective windbreak on a roof terrace.

Planting in containers If the container does have adequate drainage you will need to pie 6–12mm/¼–½in holes every 10–12cm/4–5in. Pu a layer of broken crocks or pebbles, which will all the water to drain out and prevent soil blocking holes. This layer should be a minimum of 2.5cm/ in even the smallest pot and more if your plants herbs or alpines, which need very good draina Containers for alpines should be filled with one-th crocks or pebbles followed by a layer of gravel befe the compost is added.

Then fill the container with compost, leaving gap between the surface of the compost and the of the pot of about 8cm/3in for mulch and wat Always use potting compost rather than garden s If you need to make the compost less dense add to one-quarter vermiculite or perlite, and if you ne to improve the drainage add up to half horticultu grit. All alpines and Mediterranean plants should grown in this proportion of compost and g Choosing the correct specialist compost for yo plants will help them to remain healthy in a restrict environment. Don't be tempted to reuse compost; nutrients will have been exhausted and it may carrying diseases from the previous plants.

Temporary displays will probably need to changed twice a year, in spring and autumn. Layer plants, putting large bulbs 10–15cm/4–6in deep w smaller bulbs above and annuals or biennials on to An autumn planting with tulips and daffodils at bottom, crocuses above and wallflowers (*Erysim*

cheiri) and pansies (*Viola*) at the surface will look attractive right through to the end of spring.

Care of containers After planting containers need regular feeding and watering, at least once a week in winter and once a day in summer. Containers against a wall will need watering throughout the year if they are in a rain shadow. It is important that excess water can drain away, so always make sure that the drainage holes are clear and the container raised off the ground with terracotta feet or bricks. Too much water will encourage mildew and many tender plants die in winter as a result of damp rather than frost.

Trees in containers do best if they are soaked once a week rather than given a little water every day, and they should be fed regularly with a general-purpose liquid feed. In the case of alpines, the soil should be soaked when it is quite dry.

Water a container gently until you see the water draining out of the bottom. If this happens immediately it means the plant is either dried up or pot bound. If the soil had dried up, re-soak the whole container by putting it in a bucket of water and waiting for the air bubbles to stop. You can tell if the plant is pot bound by looking for roots coming up through the surface or poking through the drainage holes. In this case you will need to re-pot the plant in a slightly larger container (it should be no larger than an extra 5cm/2in or so, or you risk shocking the plant).

Ideally all containers should be re-potted every two years. Re-potting is best done in spring when the

Below Lilies, hydrangeas and a profusion of pelargoniums, all planted in containers of various types, make use of every available corner in a sunny courtyard.

Right A window box carpeted with sedums makes a miniature garden.

temperature is not too cold and before the plant has begun its new growth. Gently tip the plant out of the container and ease the soil away from its roots, teasing them out if the plant has become pot bound. While you refill the pot, sit the plant in a bucket of diluted seaweed feed so it does not dry out. This is very important, as the roots will not benefit from the new compost if they are too dry to take in the nutrients. Fill the container with a suitable mix and replace the plant. Keep the soil damp but don't overwater. If a plant is too large to re-pot, replace the top 5cm/2in of compost only and renew the mulch. Be very careful not to damage the delicate surface roots.

Window boxes Buy the largest size of box that will fit on your sill and fix it securely with metal brackets. Simple planting schemes are the most effective, particularly if you have more than one box. Busy Lizzies, pelargoniums and petunias, for example, may look rather municipal in a bed, but are fabulous in a set of window boxes. Simple topiary is another good choice. Alternatively, make a herb box for a kitchen sill, keeping invasive mint in a separate pot.

You can create privacy with a barrier of tall plants, such as grasses and *Verbena bonariensis*. Trellis or wires stretched across the window and covered in nasturtiums or morning glory will also make an effective screen. Trailing plants look wonderful along the front of a box, cascading down the wall; put in as many as you can to create a really spectacular effect.

TRAILING PLANTS

Shrubs

Fuchsia
Hedera helix (ivy)
Helichrysum petiolare
Vinca minor (periwinkle)

Perennials

Campanula poscharskyana
Glechoma hederacea 'Variegata' (ground ivy)
Mimulus cardinalis (scarlet monkey flower)
Scaevola aemula

Annuals

Begonia
Brachyscome
Convolvulus sabatius
Diascia
Impatiens (busy Lizzie)
Lobelia erinus
Pelargonium
Petunia Surfinia Series
Thunbergia alata
Tropaeolum majus (nasturtium)
Verbena Tapien Series

Hanging baskets Hanging baskets are a good way of giving a small garden height. The bigger the basket the better, as the extra compost will conserve water and increase your choice of plants. Any annual will do well in a hanging basket and the trailing plants listed below will cascade down attractively.

Secure the basket for planting by wedging it firmly in the top of a bucket. There are various liners that you can use to hold the soil in place. Rigid basket liners conserve moisture but are not very attractive and will not let your plants grow through the mesh of the basket. They can be partly disguised with trailing plants planted around the edge of the basket, and are most suitable for baskets that will be seen from above, rather than from below. Coconut-fibre matting is a flexible option as it can be cut to fit and you can also make holes to push plants through.

A lining of sphagnum moss will give a natural look, but don't let it dry out. Line the base of the basket with 4cm/1½in of moss and push the roots of trailing plants through the mesh and moss. Add compost to cover the roots and work upwards, putting in enough plants to cover the basket. Leave a gap of 2.5cm/1in at the top of the basket for watering. Hanging baskets should not be allowed to dry out and in the summer may need watering twice a day. Wind will dry them out even faster than the sun.

Once planted and watered the basket will be very heavy, so support it well. You can reduce the weight of hanging baskets or window boxes by mixing up to one third perlite or vermiculite with the compost.

Right Globe artichoke (*Cynara cardunculus* 'Green Globe'), parsley (*Petroselinum crispum*), sweet peas (*Lathyrus odoratus*) and coneflowers (*Echinacea purpurea* 'White Swan') grow together in a roof garden.

f you have a really tiny space you are unlikely to become self-sufficient in edible foods but you will still be able to produce an interesting selection for your kitchen, perhaps with herbs in a window box, runner beans trained up a fence and strawberries in a hanging basket. The key to growing edible plants in a tiny garden is not to hide them. You won't have space for a separate vegetable patch, so incorporate the plants into the overall design. Many vegetables look as good as they taste; runner beans and tomatoes, for example, are attractive both before and after harvesting.

Pests and diseases can be a problem when you are growing edible plants as you obviously won't want to cover your future food with chemicals. Avoid encouraging disease by giving plants the correct amount of food and water and keeping fruit bushes well pruned so air can circulate through them. In many cases disease-resistant varieties are available. You can deter predators in various ways, such as netting fruit trees against the birds and growing companion plants that discourage the worst predators. (See 'Dealing with pests and diseases', page 138, for more information about environmentally friendly deterrents and cures.)

Herbs Home-grown herbs taste far better than the 'fresh' ones in a plastic bag from the supermarket and a small window box will keep your culinary needs supplied. Most herbs originate in the Mediterranean area and require sunshine and well-drained soil. Many

will survive in shade, but grown in a sunny position will have a much more intense flavour due to the oils that are brought to the surface of the leaves by sunshine. Herbs don't need much root space and do particularly well in troughs, which can be used as window boxes or placed on the ground. Adjust the soil as necessary, adding pebbles and grit for extra drainage. (See page 98 for further information on planting containers.)

Many herbs will die in winter, but parsley, mint, French tarragon and chives should all reappear in spring. Rosemary and bay are much longer lived and will eventually grow to a large size, although they can easily be kept to manageable proportions in a pot.

Herbs can be grown from seed but most are readily and cheaply available as small plants, so adopt whichever method you prefer. Buy small plants as they will settle in more quickly and within a few weeks will have grown large enough for you to harvest from them. Always plant mint in a separate pot as it will take over a large container or even a whole bed. Try to feed and water the plants regularly during the growing season, although many Mediterranean herbs are tough and will not mind if you occasionally forget them. Cold, damp conditions will do them far more harm than drought.

Pretty varieties are available that will brighten up a herb box; sage, for example, may have leaves that are purple (*Salvia officinalis* 'Purpurascens'), yellow (*S.o.* 'Kew Gold') or multi-coloured (*S.o.* 'Tricolor'), and thyme also comes in a range of colours. There's

HERBS, FRUIT & VEGETABLES

Herbs for sun

Basil (*Ocimum basilicum*)

Bay (*Laurus nobilis*)

Borage (*Borago officinalis*)

Chamomile (*Chamaemelum nobile*)

Coriander (*Coriandrum sativum*)

Dill (*Anethum graveolens*)

Fennel (*Foeniculum vulgare*)

Feverfew (*Tanacetum*)

Lavender (*Lavandula*)

Lemon balm (*Melissa officinalis*)

Marjoram, French or pot (*Origanum onites*); marjoram, sweet (*O. majorana*)

Oregano (*Origanum vulgare*)

Rosemary (*Rosmarinus officinalis*)

Sage (*Salvia officinalis*)

Tarragon (*Artemisia dracunculus*)

Thyme (*Thymus*)

Herbs for shade

Bergamot (*Monarda*)

Chervil (*Anthriscus cerefolium*)

Chives (*Allium schoenoprasum*)

Garlic (*Allium sativum*)

Mint (*Mentha*) – peppermint (*M. x piperita*); spearmint (*M. spicata*)

Parsley (*Petroselinum crispum*); parsley, Italian flat-leaf (*P.c.* var. *neapolitanum*)

also no reason why you can't mix herbs and flowers in a box or bed. Chives and parsley make good edging plants and are a change from alyssum and lobelia.

The box above lists herbs for sunny and shady sites. Herbs that thrive in shade also do well in sun.

Fruit Fruiting plants usually have two important requirements that your site must satisfy: shelter from the wind and a certain amount of sunshine. Spring is a risky time for fruit as frost can damage the buds and destroy the harvest, so if you live in an area prone to late spring frosts either choose late-flowering varieties or be prepared to protect the plant with fleece during cold weather.

Fruit trees are particularly suitable for tiny gardens because you can choose the final size the plant will reach. This is because nearly all fruit trees are grafted on to rootstocks rather than grown from seeds or cuttings. By selecting the appropriate rootstock and graft you can (within reason) have the fruit you want on a tree that will fit in your garden. Choose a fruit variety that is disease resistant and, if you only have room for one plant, reliably self-pollinating. You can select a rootstock that will enable you to grow the plant in a container or train it flat against a sunny wall. Training a fruit tree as a fan or espalier will give you blossom in spring, fruit in summer or autumn and an interesting shape in winter, and the wall will protect the plant from harsh weather.

Apple rootstocks for a small space are 'M27', which is very dwarf (maximum 1.8m/6ft), 'M9', which is

dwarf (2.5m/8ft), or 'M26' and 'MM106', which are semi-dwarf or half standard (4.8m/16ft). You can have a single-stem flagpole or ballerina tree. The numbering refers to the trials that established the most reliable rootstocks. Apples like well-drained soil and sun, and do well against a south- or west-facing wall.

Pears are at risk from frost damage as they flower early, so should only be grown in warm or sheltered areas. Quince rootstocks are used for pear trees and 'Quince A' (4.5m/15ft) or 'Quince C' (3m/10ft) are the ones to choose. The smallest, 'Quince C', must have good soil. 'EMH' is a new rootstock between A and C and combines the advantages of both.

Cherries blossom late and are only slightly at risk from frost, but need a sunny spot. The exceptions are Morello cherries (*Prunus cerasus*), which will grow in shade or against an east-facing wall. Rootstocks to choose are 'Inmil' (1.8m/6ft), 'Damil' (4.5m/15ft) or 'Colt' (6m/20ft). Plums on 'Pixy' (4.5m/15ft) or 'St Julien A' (4.5m/15ft), peaches and nectarines on 'St Julien A' (4.5m/15ft) or 'Brompton' (6m/20ft) and apricots (*Prunus armeniaca*) on 'St Julien A' (4.5m/15ft) can all be grown against a sunny wall. Quinces also grow in a sunny site. Choose *Chaenomeles* 'Vranja' for frost resistance.

Oranges, lemons and olives are best grown in pots that can be protected from cold and damp. Figs also need protection from cold as the fruit overwinters on the plant and ripens the following summer. Figs fruit best with constrained roots, so bury a container in the ground or put paving slabs around the roots to

Below, top Strawberries (*Fragaria* 'Gorella') in tiny pots.

Below, bottom Sweetcorn (*Zea mays*) and lettuce (*Lactuca sativa*) in a bed cut from the decking.

Opposite, top Apples on cordons.

Opposite, bottom A window box planted with alpine strawberries (*Fragaria vesca* 'Semperflorens'), variegated ground ivy (*Glechoma hederacea* 'Variegata'), *Pelargonium* 'Lady Plymouth', and herbs including French lavender (*Lavandula stoechas*), chives (*Allium schoenoprasum*), gold-variegated sage (*Salvia officinalis* 'Icterina'), fennel (*Foeniculum vulgare*), variegated lemon balm (*Melissa officinalis* 'Aurea'), golden feverfew (*Tanacetum parthenium* 'Aureum') and chamomile (*Chamaemelum nobile*).

create a space 45cm/18in deep and wide. 'Brown Turkey' and 'White Marseilles' are the hardiest varieties.

You can grow soft fruits instead of ornamental plants, either as bushes or climbers. Gooseberries can be grown as a cordon against a wall or as a bush, and do well in shade. If they have sunshine, blackcurrants and redcurrants will also be very happy against a wall. Cane fruits include raspberries, blackberries and crosses such as loganberries and tayberries. They can all be grown as climbers and will thrive in sun or light shade, but raspberries are not particularly decorative and blackberries grow very large.

Strawberries are suitable for even the smallest space as they can be grown in pots, window boxes or hanging baskets. They need good soil drainage and plenty of sunshine. Alpine strawberries (*Fragaria vesca* 'Semperflorens') are especially useful in a confined area as they form neat clumps and flower up to the first frosts. Grape vines are easy to grow, but require a lot of space and a hot, dry autumn to ripen. In a tiny garden they can be trained across trellis, from where they will hang and create a pleasant dappled shade.

Vegetables You can easily accommodate vegetables in a small garden as long as you choose varieties to suit the space. Runner beans, for example, also have an ornamental function, quickly covering an area with foliage and providing attractive red flowers – and as a bonus you get the beans. Like other tall vegetables they can be grown against a wall or fence to take up

VEGETABLES FOR A TINY GARDEN

Vegetables for containers

Beetroot (*Beta vulgaris*)

Dwarf beans (*Phaseolus vulgaris*)

Carrot (*Daucus carota*)

Chives (*Allium schoenoprasum*)

Cucumber (*Cucumis sativus*)

Garlic (*Allium sativum*)

Lettuce (*Lactuca sativa*)

Onion, shallot (*Allium*)

Potatoes (*Solanum tuberosum*)

Radish (*Raphanus sativus*)

Sorrel (*Rumex*)

Spinach (*Spinacea oleracea*)

Sweet pepper, chilli (*Capsicum*)

Swiss chard (*Beta vulgaris* subsp. *cicla*)

Tomato (*Lycopersicon esculentum*)

Vegetables for a wall

French beans (*Phaseolus vulgaris*)

Runner beans (*P. coccineus*)

Courgettes (*Cucurbita pepo*)

Cucumbers (*Cucumis sativus*)

Sweet pepper, chilli (*Capsicum*)

Tomato (*Lycopersicon esculentum*)

minimum room. Tomatoes, chillies, cucumbers and gourds can all be grown against a sunny wall and if the garden is sheltered should ripen successfully.

Many root crops are suitable for containers. Plant small-rooted varieties, such as spherical carrots or baby beetroot, in as large a pot as possible. Taller plants such as tomatoes, cucumbers and chard also do well in containers. French and runner beans will produce a better crop if planted in a bed, but dwarf beans do not mind being grown in pots.

Inter-cropping is a method used in intensive horticulture which can be adapted to make the most of a small bed. It involves planting a small, quick-growing crop amongst a slower one, which will fill the holes left when you harvest the first crop. Lettuces, radishes and rocket work well as in-between plants with carrots, brassicas or flowers growing more slowly.

You can also use vegetables as an edging, lining a flowerbed with lettuces, radishes, carrots or spinach. Harvest carefully, re-sowing as you crop, and you will not spoil your display. Swiss chard (*Beta vulgaris* subsp. *cicla*) is a very attractive plant with striking red, yellow or white stems; 'Rhubarb Chard' and 'Vulcan' are particularly brilliant. Growing certain flowers and edible plants together can actually reduce pests. Marigolds deter aphids and whitefly, for example, while onions and garlic discourage greenfly (aphids).

If you grow vegetables in a bed, feed the soil well and avoid putting the same plants in the same place year after year. This will help to prevent disease and depletion of the soil.

WATER
FEATURES

Left A lemon tree flourishes in a pot positioned in the pool that occupies almost the whole of a tiny courtyard in Andalucia. The lower parts of the trunk and branches have been coated with chalk, which is traditionally used as an insect deterrent in this part of Spain.

A water feature is one of the easiest things to include in a tiny garden and can make a huge difference to the ambience of the space. Still or slowly dripping water is very restful, while fountains tend to create a more exhilarating effect, cooling the air and dazzling as they catch the sunlight in an exposed site. The sound of falling water will also distract from background noise such as passing traffic.

There is a wide range of ready-made water features available, some with a submersible pump included. If you don't like any of these consider creating your own, perhaps from a half barrel or a stone trough. You may not have room for a properly wild pond, but even a barrel containing a few plants will attract wildlife.

Movement catches the eye and a fountain, however small, will become the focal point of the garden. In a small area, a simple water feature with a single jet or fall of water may be the most effective. Check the prevailing wind before you position a tall jet or you may end up with water being blown all over your sitting area or into the house.

Still water will reflect light on a bright, sunny day, but on dull days it will appear bleak and grey and do little to enhance your garden, particularly in winter. The solution is to break up the surface, perhaps with plants, stones or jets of water produced by underwater pumps. These jets need not be large; in a garden this size we are talking a few inches, not several hundred feet!

You can add an extra sparkle, and increase the perceived size of the pool, by putting up a mirror that reflects sunlight and water. It is also worth considering some sort of lighting to make the most of the feature at night. You could either have an underwater light installed or shine a light on to the feature from above.

If you have children, safety is an important aspect to consider. Shallow water bubbling over stones or pebbles will give you the sound and movement of water without the risk. This type of feature can be incorporated in the smallest space and suits most styles of garden. Water bubbling up through the centre of millstones, for example, is particularly attractive, and you can buy boulders with holes drilled through them for this purpose.

Another type of feature that can be suitable if you have small children or very limited space is a wall-mounted spout. These will fit into the tiniest garden and there is a huge range of styles, from formal stone lion heads to simple Japanese-style wooden pipes. Most have a container at ground level that holds the reservoir of water and the pump, and a pipe that carries water up to the spout. You can disguise the pipe by building a false wall or training plants in front of it.

If you have enough space you could build a permanent pond, either against a wall or sunk into the ground. Raised pools are more economical in terms of space, especially if you build thick retaining walls that can double as seats. Always ensure that a

Right *Schoenoplectus lacustris* subsp. *tabernaemontani* 'Zebrinus', *Astelia chathamica* and ferns luxuriate in a lush water garden on a tiny terrace.

pool is leak-proof by putting down a layer of sand, and then one of impermeable geo-textile such as butyl, before laying the concrete. The butyl will prevent leaks even if the concrete cracks and the sand will protect the butyl from sharp stones in the ground.

Free-standing features are easy to maintain and move around. You can use any container as long as it is watertight. In addition to the more usual terracotta or stone, consider materials such as glass, stainless steel or acrylic. A half barrel makes a good pond; if you soak it well the wood should expand and make the barrel watertight, but as an extra measure line it with heavy-duty polythene. Do not use barrels that have been used to hold oil, tar, wood preservative or creosote.

Water plants If you want to grow plants in a pond or other water feature, you will need to position it so it is in the sun and choose plants suitable for the depth of water. If you want fish, the pond must be at least 60cm/24in deep and provide some shade, either with plants or a solid overhang. Fish are hard to keep successfully in a small volume of water.

Water plants are categorized according to their preferred root depth. Deep-water aquatics have their roots at the bottom of the pool (usually at a depth of 25cm/10in) and their leaves on the surface. Many have attractive leaves and flowers, water lilies being the most common. Submerged plants live entirely under water. They oxygenate the water and prevent algae growing. Floating plants behave exactly as you

MARGINAL PLANTS

Sun

Astelia chathamica
Myosotis scorpioides 'Mermaid'
Zantedeschia aethiopica (arum lily)

Sun/part shade

Caltha palustris (marsh marigold)
Iris laevigata
I. pseudacorus (yellow flag iris)
I. versicolor (blue flag iris)
Schoenoplectus lacustris subsp.
   tabernaemontani 'Zebrinus'
Typha minima (miniature bulrush)

SUBMERGED PLANTS

Sun

Hottonia palustris (water violet)
Lagarosiphon major
   (curly water thyme)
Myriophyllum verticillatum (milfoil)

Sun/part shade

Callitriche hermaphroditica syn.
   C. autumnalis (autumn starwort)
Potamogeton crispus (curled
   pondweed)
Ranunculus aquatilis (water crowfoot)

FLOATING PLANTS

Sun

Eichhornia crassipes (water hyacinth)
Hydrocharis morsus-ranae (frogbit)
Pistia stratiotes (water lettuce)
Salvinia auriculata (butterfly fern)
Stratiotes aloides (water soldier)

Sun/part shade

Azolla filiculoides (fairy moss)

un

enyanthes trifoliata (bogbean)
ontium aquaticum
    (golden club)
mphaea (water lily)
N. 'Aurora' – apricot to
    red; *N.* 'Charlene
    Strawn' – yellow,
    fragrant; *N.* 'Ellisiana' –
    red; *N.* x *helvola* – yellow;
    N. 'Gonnère' – white,
    fragrant; *N.* 'James
    Brydon' – red;

N. 'Pink Sensation' –
    pink; *N. tetragona* var.
    rubra – red
Nymphoides peltata
    (yellow floating heart)

Sun/shade
Aponogeton distachyos
    (water hawthorn)

Opposite Water lilies (*Nymphaea tetragona*) flourish in a small raised pool on a decked terrace.

Below A simple fountain composed of a bamboo spout and stone bowl surrounded by pebbles makes an effective feature in the tiniest of corners.

uld expect, trailing their roots just below the surface of water. They will create shade and discourage algae.
rginal plants like their roots wet but their leaves dry, grow in shallow water (usually up to 15cm/6in). They be grown in deeper water by raising up their ntainers on bricks. Specially designed planting kets are a good idea even if you have a soil-based nd, as they will restrict growth and stop plants coming invasive.

The boxes on this page provide a selection of water nts suitable for a small pond or water feature. The ting plants *Hydrocharis morsus-ranae* (frogbit) and atiotes aloides* (water soldier) are both hardy, but tend be invasive. The other floating plants are not hardy usually best grown as annuals.

intenance Any shallow water in sunlight will turn udy and green due to the growth of algae, but having nts in your pond will keep the water clear. The water y turn cloudy while the plants are settling in, but it will ntually clear. Do not clean the water during this time you will simply delay the settling of the plants.

If you do not have plants or fish you can use an ultra-et filter or put a chemical solution in the water to bit the growth of algae. If using chemicals ensure that child or animal can drink from the pond. Alternatively, clean a small water feature as and when the algae ds up; it comes off easily with a scrubbing brush.

During winter, remove fallen leaves and break any ice t begins to form. A small feature without plants could ply be dismantled, cleaned and put away until spring.

FURNITURE
ORNAMENT

n a tiny garden elements such as lighting, furniture and decoration will contribute as much to the overall look of the space as the plants. A quirky bench or a stone statue will be on show throughout the year and provide a major focal point, especially in winter when few plants are flowering. You can also play around with lighting, mirrors and *trompe l'oeil* to influence the mood of the garden and even create an illusion of spaciousness.

Furniture and storage A table and chairs may be the largest objects in your garden, so it's worth going for something interesting. Folding tables and chairs can be put away when not in use but you will need somewhere to store them, so furniture that stays in place all year round may actually be a more practical option. If you are leaving furniture outside, treat all wood other than renewable hardwood with preservative and metal other than aluminium with specialist metal paint.

However tiny your garden, you will need somewhere to store your tools and equipment. A watering can may look charming if left out when not in use, but few other tools can double up as ornaments. Storing them in an old bucket is one practical but not particularly attractive option. A trug or other type of basket, on the other hand, will hold everything and look attractive as well.

If possible you need an area where you can hide away pots, unused compost and mulch. A small shed is very useful, but you may well not have

sufficient room for it. If this is the case, consider a bench with built-in storage space underneath or a lidded box that could double as a seat. Another option is to have a shallow shed built up against a wall. This will take up much less room than a free-standing shed and will still protect your tools and keep them out of sight. You can either make a feature of the shed by painting it attractively or hide it using climbers – a pot on either side with ivy and jasmine would soon create a screen. Even on a balcony a sentry box like this can justify the space it takes up and become a feature in its own right.

If you want to grow a lot of plants from seed you will need a mini greenhouse or propagator, which can be bought as small as 30cm/12in x 90cm/36in. In a small garden it is important that this looks attractive as well as being useful. Tiny portable greenhouses are available from garden centres and DIY shops, and need not be an eyesore if you keep them clean and tidy. One or two flowering plants such as pelargoniums in pots will greatly enhance the overall appearance.

Lighting Avoid having too many sources of light, as this will detract from the overall effect. You could illuminate steps or a path with low-level lighting or train a spotlight on a single focal point. You could also position a light behind an object such as an architectural plant to highlight the silhouette. A spotlight with its beam directed downwards could even be used to mimic moonlight shining through a tree. In a small urban space, artificial light can be

Previous page The curves of a stone seat-sculpture mimic the sweep of the decking.

Below Dark-toned decking and wicker furniture in a basement area create the sense of an in-between garden that seems to be part of the house.

Opposite, top In a tiny garden storage needs are often best solved vertically.

Opposite, bottom A simple colour scheme links benches, chairs, table and decking, and the benches double up as garden storage.

angled to make the surroundings seem much darker than they really are.

A light to deter intruders should obviously be as bright as possible, but for most other garden lighting soft, low-voltage lights work best. The shadows are as important as the light itself – it's not necessary to illuminate the entire garden.

Solar-powered lights store energy from the sun during the day and make good garden illumination as they have no cables and can easily be moved around. Although not very bright, they are an attractive, flexible and safe source of lighting.

Candles and garden flares aren't particularly bright, but are perfectly adequate to eat by and very atmospheric. There are many different types of lantern available; even an ordinary candle in a jam jar will look lovely. Any candle needs to be set on a heat-proof surface, away from overhanging branches. Citronella candles have the double benefit of giving light and deterring mosquitoes. Fairy lights in the branches of a tree or night lights dotted around the base of the plants will not create much light, but will be enchanting on a warm summer's evening.

Ornaments and illusions Even though your garden is small scale, your decoration need not be. As a rule, one decent-sized ornament looks better than several small ones. You can use anything, from an antique stone statue to a piece of driftwood. Ornaments draw attention to themselves, so are useful for filling spaces and directing the eye around the space.

Architectural plants can be treated as an ornamental focal point, as can topiary or plants trained around a wire frame. (See page 122 for a selection of architectural plants.)

Mirrors or *trompe l'oeil* are excellent means of making a tiny garden seem much larger or producing the illusion that more garden, or even countryside, lies just the other side of the wall. Before installing a mirror seal the edges with silicone or yacht varnish to protect the silvering from moisture. Perspex also provides a reflective surface and is safer to use over large areas. If you want a less direct reflection, try a layer of aluminium foil sandwiched between a sheet of glass and a plywood backing. Galvanized metal, beaten copper and zinc can be used to create light and shadow rather than reflect exact images. They will not necessarily make your garden seem much larger, but will brighten a dark corner.

Avoid positioning a container or ornament right up against the glass, as the obvious reflection will spoil the illusion. To complete the deception, hide the edges of the mirror completely with plants or a fake doorway or arch.

A *trompe l'oeil* fresco can be used to create the illusion of any scene you want beyond your garden boundary. Again, you can disguise the edges using a false doorway or window frame, perhaps creating the impression that your garden extends through a mysterious gateway or looks out on a scene of rolling hills and cornfields.

Train spotlights to emphasize the contours of plants and block
out the world beyond, or use a combination of spotlights and
ordinary candles in jars to light up the leaves from below.

Outdoor lighting can be as theatrical as you wish: install an
elaborate chandelier filled with tiny candles or suspend fairy
lights from branches and overhead wires.

ARCHITECTURAL PLANTS

Acanthus spinosus
  (bear's breeches)
Aeonium 'Zwartkop'
  syn. *A.* 'Schwarzkopf'
Agapanthus (African blue lily)
Agave americana 'Marginata'
A. parviflora
Allium – especially *A. christophii*
Carex elata 'Aurea' (Bowles'
  golden sedge)
Cordyline australis (New Zealand
  cabbage palm)
Cynara cardunculus (cardoon)
Eryngium (sea holly)
Euphorbia characias subsp.
  wulfenii (spurge)
Fargesia murieliae syn.
  Arundinaria murieliae
  (umbrella bamboo)
F. nitida syn. *A. nitida*
  (fountain bamboo)

Fatsia japonica
Festuca glauca (blue fescue)
Fritillaria imperialis
Helianthus annuus (sunflower)
Hosta – especially *H. sieboldiana*
  var. *elegans*
Ilex aquifolium (holly)
Juniperus scopulorum 'Skyrocket'
Kniphofia
Lilium regale (lily)
Melianthus major (honey bush)
Miscanthus sinensis
Olea europaea (olive)
Phormium cookianum
  (mountain flax)
P. tenax 'Dazzler' (New
  Zealand flax)
Phyllostachys aurea
  (fishpole bamboo)
Sedum morganianum
Yucca filamentosa

Opposite, top A monumental urn towers above clipped box balls.

Opposite, bottom A griffin lurks among asparagus, hostas and ferns.

Left Screened by overhanging roses, a mirror hints at another garden extending beyond the door.

Below A *trompe l'oeil* mural turns the blank wall outside a window into a sweeping vista.

I n a really tiny garden, the surface area of the walls or fences will almost certainly be greater than the ground area. For this reason it is important to make the most of your garden's boundaries: they can be used not only to create privacy and shelter but also as an opportunity for decoration. Painting them different colours will change the atmosphere of the space, while mirrors or *trompe l'oeil* will give an illusion of greater space (see page 117). Most importantly, these surfaces can be used to support climbing plants that will provide you

with greenery, flowers and berries without the bulk of a large shrub.

Walls, fences and trellis are usually more suitable for a tiny garden than hedging, as a hedge is very bulky and will use up all the nutrients in the soil. The exception is a front garden that may contain nothing but a hedge.

Walls are long lasting and can be very beautiful, but putting one up is expensive. In order to last a wall ideally needs proper foundations, a damp course and coping along the top to prevent rainwater seeping in between the bricks and mortar. To act as an effective windbreak the wall may need to be extended with a semi-permeable barrier such as trellis, which will slow down wind rather than simply channelling it over the top of the wall.

Some plants, such as ivy, will cling to a wall, but most will need wires or trellis to twine around. If you paint the wall wires may be the more practical option, as you can detach them when repainting. Walls with plants are usually best left unpainted or so covered with greenery that you cannot see when the paintwork gets shabby.

Walls absorb heat during the day and release it at night, which will help create a warm micro-climate within your garden. As long as the space is also sheltered from strong winds, you will be able to grow more tender plants than if you had a fence or hedge.

One or more of your walls may form the side of another building, in which case it will probably be high and oppressive. This effect can be reduced by

CES

Opposite In the absence of a flowerbed, the owner of this roadside property has simply pulled up the cobblestones and piled them to make a decorative cairn. A cascade of ivy (*Hedera*) drops down the side of the house to the cairn.

Below The painted city skyline disguises the height of the wall, drawing the eye down into the garden.

creating a demarcation line with paint, decorative trellis or plants at about 1.8m/6ft, to produce the illusion that the wall ends there. You can also use wall-mounted containers to break up the expanse of brickwork and add colour and interest.

Fences are cheaper than walls and also take up much less space. Closeboard fencing of vertical planks nailed to cross-rails is the best choice if you want privacy and a solid support for plants. If you are going to grow plants along a fence it should be firmly secured in place with vertical supports fixed in concrete or metal spikes embedded in the soil. The plants can be trained along wires attached to the fence.

Trellis allows through more light and air than a solid fence or wall, and still gives privacy. It can be used as an openwork fence, or as a support or decoration in front of a fence or wall, or as a vertical extension to a solid barrier. Ready-made panels come in a range of sizes. Expanding trellis is not as strong, but can be stretched along a fence or wall to give a diamond-shaped latticework covering and will support small climbers. You can paint trellis any colour you like, but repainting will not be easy if there are plants growing along it. White will make the trellis really stand out, but is suitable only if you can repaint at regular intervals. Natural or dark colours may be more appropriate for trellis supporting plants as these colours will recede into the background and let the plants look their best.

Ideally trellis should be positioned 2.5cm/1in away from the fence or wall, to allow room for the

CLIMBERS & WALL PLANTS

Sun

Abutilon megapotamicum
Actinidia kolomikta
Bougainvillea
Campsis radicans (trumpet vine)
Clematis
Fruit, fanned or espaliered
Jasminum officinale (summer jasmine)
Solanum crispum 'Glasnevin'
Vitis 'Brant' (edible grape)
V. coignetiae (crimson glory vine)
V. vinifera (grape vine)

Lonicera (honeysuckle)
Parthenocissus henryana (Chinese Virginia creeper)
Passiflora caerulea (passion flower)
Pyracantha
Tropaeolum speciosum (flame nasturtium)
Wisteria sinensis

Sun/part shade

Akebia quinata (chocolate vine)
Humulus lupulus 'Aureus' (golden hop)
Jasminum x stephanense
Lathyrus latifolius (perennial pea)

Any

Clematis viticella
Hedera (ivy)
Jasminum nudiflorum (winter jasmine)
Parthenocissus quinquefolia (Virginia creeper)
Rosa (rose) – position depends on cultivar

ANNUAL CLIMBERS

Sun

Cobaea scandens (cup and saucer vine)
Eccremocarpus scaber (Chilean glory flower)
Ipomoea purpurea/I. tricolor (morning glory)
Tropaeolum majus (nasturtium)

Sun/part shade

Lathyrus odoratus (sweet pea)
Runner beans

Below left Trellis provides screening in a city garden.

Below Echeveria, agave and sempervivum grow in a planting box fixed to the top of a wall.

Bottom Baked bean tins planted with *Sutera cordata* make a novel wall decoration.

Left This tiny space has all the elements of a romantic garden – trellis, roses, lavender and clipped box.

plants to twine around it and air to circulate. Nail wooden spacers of the right size to the garden boundary to create an even gap, and then fix the trellis to that. Trellis must be very firmly secured otherwise the weight of the plants will pull it down. This is especially true if you are using trellis as a vertical extension to a wall or fence; use long posts embedded in the ground as supports.

Bricks and wood are not the only options for your boundaries. Other choices include metal railings in a formal front garden, concrete blocks as an alternative to bricks, or woven willow and hazel hurdles instead of fencing. Glass or plastic are particularly useful for roof gardens or balconies where you need shelter but do not want to block the view.

The group of climbers divides into self-clinging plants such as ivy or Virginia creeper (*Parthenocissus quinquefolia*), which use rootlets to hold on with, and those like peas with tendrils that cling on to trellis or wire. Honeysuckle and summer jasmine (*Jasminum officinale*) wind themselves around the support while climbers with straight stems, such as roses, winter jasmine (*Jasminum nudiflorum*) and Chilean potato vine (*Solanum crispum*), need to be tied in place and trained to a framework.

When you are clothing your boundary surfaces with plants, take care to choose a mix that will offer both seasonal interest and year-round cover. Clematis and roses go particularly well together, giving you flowers from early spring right through to mid-winter. Vary the colour and shape of the leaves,

remembering that large-leaved plants can make an area seem smaller as they push inwards.

Some climbing plants may grow too large for a tiny space. Russian vine (*Fallopia baldschuanica*) is often guilty of outgrowing its allotted space and taking over the whole garden – in fact, its other common name is mile-a-minute! You can regularly trim plants such as ivy to keep them under control, but hard pruning can encourage a plant to grow even more. It is possible to limit a plant by growing it in a container, but most climbers are happier if their roots are in open soil.

If your garden is paved it may be possible to remove a paving slab and plant the climber. Dig out the stone and rubble and replace it with a suitable compost mix. If the soil is very poor, grow the plant in a pot with the bottom knocked out. By the time the roots reach the ground they will be sufficiently established to be able to work their way through the poorer soil. Mix some compost in the soil below and put some soil into the container so the plant will not notice the transition from pot to ground.

On page 126 there is a selection of plants that can be grown against walls. Many of the annuals are actually tender perennials or shrubs and may survive longer in a frost-free area. All climbers need a certain amount of guidance and wall shrubs in particular will require regular tying-in to train them. (See page 138 for information about training plants.)

KEEP
GA
LOOK

MAINTAINING A TINY GARDEN

Although there is no such thing as a 'no-maintenance' garden, the good news is that very small spaces will require on average a total of only half an hour of care a week and often less than that in winter. The most important aspect of looking after a tiny garden is to give your plants the best chance you can from the start. If you don't have room for many specimens you want those you do have to perform longer than they would naturally, so it's a good idea to help them as much as possible. This means making sure that the soil is good and the plants suitable for the conditions of your garden. Don't ask the impossible of your plants; if you are not able to water regularly, for example, choose plants that are drought-tolerant.

Buy the best quality of plants you can. Annuals, in particular, need to perform quickly and an ailing annual is unlikely to recover in time to justify its position in a very small garden. If you are buying a tree or specimen shrub it is a good idea to go to a specialist nursery, but for most perennials, annuals and bulbs it does not really matter where you buy them as long as they are healthy. Markets and local shops may not offer such a wide choice, but there is no reason why the individual plants should not be as good as those from a nursery.

As a general rule, check that the plant you are buying is held firmly inside the pot and that its roots are not poking out the bottom. If they are, the plant is best avoided as it will already be stressed. The compost should be damp rather than soggy, and the plant should look healthy. It is usually a good idea to buy smaller plants as they are cheaper and will usually settle in more quickly than larger specimens, growing faster in the long run. Buying plants, particularly annuals, in bud is usually best, as the plant will be able to settle in and then flower.

While it does no harm to fill your garden to capacity, the plants should not be overcrowded. If you put too many plants in a confined space they will simply become tall and leggy in a desperate attempt to outgrow their neighbours, and in the long run many may die.

Once you have put in the plants, the trick with maintenance is little and often. Major jobs, such as mulching, pruning and planting up containers, are obviously governed by the seasons, but all small tasks yield better results if carried out on a regular basis. Containers in particular need watering most days during summer, and at the same time you can deadhead, tie in or stake as necessary.

Regular maintenance will also allow you to spot and deal with potential problems before they become serious. Aim to water plants before they wilt, feed them before the soil becomes starved and trim them before they take over the garden. Weeds and greenfly will invade most gardens given half a chance, but can easily be controlled if you deal with them regularly as and when they appear (see page 138).

If you really want to save maintenance time and have space for a bed, avoid using containers and fill the bed with slow-growing shrubs and bulbs, which will largely manage on their own once established.

TOOLS FOR A TINY GARDEN

With a garden of this size you will need few tools and probably no machinery at all. Even a small patch of lawn is better cut with shears than a mower.

Hand trowel and hand fork These are likely to be the tools you use most often and it is worth investing in the best quality you can afford. Tools with stainless-steel blades and wooden handles are more expensive than those made of carbon steel and plastic, but will last much longer and are a joy to use. Narrow-bladed trowels are particularly useful for putting small plants into a bed that is already fairly full.

Fork and spade These come in two sizes, digging and border. Border forks and spades are narrower and will probably be all you need, if you need them at all. Consider how much use you will get out of them and buy accordingly.

Secateurs These are absolutely vital and it is worth buying a good-quality pair as they will be easier to use than cheaper models and much more durable. Secateurs should be comfortable to hold, cut up to 1cm/^{1}/$_2$in with no effort and have a safety catch to close the blades. They are available with either straight or curved blades. The straight blade can leave a ragged cut, but the sort of blade you choose really boils down to personal preference and the model you find easiest to use. Florists' scissors are handy for deadheading delicate plants, particularly annuals, when secateurs can be clumsy and awkward to use.

Hose/watering can For any space bigger than a window box, an outdoor tap will make life much easier. Whether you use a hose or watering can is up to you. If you have a hose, save storage space by putting up a wall-mounted holder or hook. If you are away a lot or have a roof garden, it is worth installing an irrigation system (see page 135).

General equipment You are unlikely to need any other specialist equipment. Hoes, rakes and barrows are simply unnecessary in a tiny garden. A pruning saw, shears or a bulb planter may be useful, depending on the type of plants you have, and a pair of stout gloves will protect your hands when pruning roses.

What you will need is a number of odds and ends that are not exactly tools. Many plants need some sort of support, so you will require a selection of different sizes of stakes or canes. Pea sticks and natural branches can look more attractive than canes but in a confined space it is usually more practical to use simple sticks, perhaps painting them brown or green to help them blend into the background. String or ties are necessary to hold the plants in place. String does not last as long as wire or plastic, but is less likely to cut into the growing plant and looks more natural.

Simple sprayers holding ^{1}/$_2$–1 litre/1–2 pints of water are useful for spraying a gentle mist over young or delicate plants. They can also be used for spraying soapy water on to greenfly or for insecticides. Always use different sprayers for each substance and label them clearly; your young seedlings will not appreciate a soapy bath and will probably die if soaked with insecticide.

You will need a dustpan and brush, and possibly a broom, to keep the garden tidy. Besoms are witches' broomsticks made of twigs tied to a larger stick and look attractive enough to be left on show when not in use, thereby solving the storage problem. (For more suggestions on where to keep your tools and equipment, see page 115.)

Always clean your tools and dry them before you put them away, oiling secateurs if necessary. This will only take a couple of moments, but will ensure your tools look good and last longer.

PREPARING THE SOIL AND PLANTING

If you are going to expect a lot from your plants, it's a good idea to ensure they are well planted in good soil. You can buy suitable compost for containers, but before you plant anything directly into the ground it is worth taking time to ensure the soil is in tip-top condition. In a tiny garden there is really no excuse not to do this and a little work at the beginning will reward you with years of healthy and productive plants. While it is not worth trying to change the basic acidity or alkalinity of the soil, you can certainly do a lot to improve its drainage and structure. Plants may last for a while in poor soil, but they will never reach their full potential.

Soil preparation Remove any rubbish, large stones or lumps of rubble and then dig the soil over. Digging over is particularly important if the earth is compacted as it will separate out the individual soil particles.

Before buying any plants, check whether the soil is acid or alkaline using a pH tester as described on page 10. Many plants are not affected by the acidity or alkalinity of the soil, but some will only tolerate certain conditions.

You also need to find out how quickly your soil drains. Dig a hole the size of a spade's blade, fill it with water and see what happens. If the water sits in the hole for more than half an hour then your plants will be sitting in water too, and many, particularly those of Mediterranean origin, will not be happy. Equally, if the water drains away immediately there is a risk that the nutrients in the soil will simply be washed away every time it rains or you water.

The texture and rate of drainage of the soil is largely determined by the amount of sand or clay present. Too much clay means the topsoil stays cold, can get waterlogged in wet weather and tends to dry out and crack during dry spells. Too much sand means the soil cannot hold water at all and any nutrients tend to be washed straight through.

The amount of sand or clay in the topsoil is governed by the bedrock far below, but the structure of the topsoil can usually be improved fairly successfully. Apart from large trees and shrubs, most plants will keep their roots in the upper layer of soil and unless this is very shallow you do not have to worry too much about the state of the subsoil. Digging in organic material in the form of compost or well-rotted manure will increase the fertility of both clay and sandy soils, and prevent excessively fast drainage, and if your soil is very sticky and drains poorly you can benefit it by adding sand or horticultural grit. You should aim for a crumbly mixture that you can run your fingers through easily.

It is important to distinguish between the nutrients in the soil and the structure. Adding packet or liquid fertilizers, such as blood, fish and bone or seaweed food (see page 136 for more on feeding), will improve the nutritional value of the soil but will do nothing to help its structure. Once your soil has a good structure it will be able to make the most of the food and water you give it. A good structure will also enable earthworms to move about more freely and they, in turn, will improve the soil even more.

In a small town garden, a greater influence than the nature of the bedrock on the quality of the topsoil may be the quantity of builders' waste and rubble present. If you have just one flowerbed it may be possible to replace all the soil, but make sure you buy from a reputable supplier as you don't want to find that your new soil is full of stones and weeds.

PLANTS OR SEEDS?

Trees, shrubs and some perennials – such as acanthus, bleeding heart (Dicentra spectabilis), aconitum and peony – are best bought as young plants as they grow slowly from seed and can be hard to germinate. With other perennials and many annuals you have the choice of buying plants or growing your own from seed.

Different seeds have different requirements. Some need darkness or warmth (or both) to germinate and others have to be planted in situ as they do not like being disturbed. Seeds can be grown in trays, pots, plugs or root trainers. Whatever container you use, it should have good drainage and hold at least 4cm/1½in of compost. Plants that have long roots, such as sweet peas, should be grown in deeper pots or root trainers.

Soak the compost or wait for the plugs to swell up and allow any excess water to drain away before you plant the seeds. Plant at the correct depth and follow any instructions regarding temperature and light. Above all do not overwater the seedlings. More than two-thirds of seedlings die from damping off, a problem caused by an excess of water.

Once the seedlings grow two or more sets of true leaves (rather than the first, false pair that appears) they can be re-potted into larger containers if necessary. When they are fully grown into young plants they can be planted in their permanent positions.

PLANTING TREES AND SHRUBS

Trees and shrubs are sold either in containers or with their roots and soil wrapped in sacking (bare rooted). If the plant does not come in a container you must put it into the soil straight away to stop the roots drying out. The traditional way to plant trees and shrubs is to dig a large deep hole and mix a generous quantity of organic matter in with the soil. The theory is that the rich surroundings will encourage the roots to spread out and down. An alternative method now being encouraged is based on the fact that 90 per cent of all tree and shrub roots are in the top 30cm/12in of soil. The theory of saucer planting, as this method is called, is that too much richness actually inhibits the growth of roots, as there is no incentive for them to stretch out in search of food. As a result the plant is less well anchored in the soil and less able to cope when the initial supply of nutrients is exhausted. Saucer planting is, however, unlikely to be practical in a restricted space as it is based on the excavation of a shallow circle 60cm/24in around the plant.

In a very small garden the best method is probably to dig a hole that is deep and wide enough to easily accommodate the roots. Try to loosen the soil around and below the hole so the roots will be able to penetrate it easily. Add a handful of bonemeal or some fertilizer, and dig in sand if the soil is poorly drained. Ensure that both the plant and the soil are damp, but not sodden. Then spread out the roots in the hole if planting a bare-rooted plant, or gently tease out the roots of a container plant. Insert a stake if necessary, fill in the hole with soil and water well. Once the soil is damp apply a layer of mulch, such as composted bark, up to 5cm/2in around the stem to suppress weeds and conserve water.

Climbers should be planted in the same way, leaving at least 30cm/12in between the wall and the plant. This is because the soil at the base of any wall may be in a rain shadow and anyway tends to be very dry. After planting untie the stems and gently train them where you want them to go, using soft twine and allowing room for the stems to grow.

Most container-grown trees and shrubs can be planted at any time of year. Roses and bare-rooted plants tend to do best if planted between late autumn and early spring. What is important is that you keep the plant well watered for the first two years while it is settling in and establishing its root system.

PLANTING PERENNIALS, BIENNIALS AND ANNUALS

These can all be planted following the same principles as for trees and shrubs, but remember that they may be very delicate. Annuals, in particular, should always be lifted by the leaves or rootball so the main stem is not damaged. Perennials are usually best planted in spring or autumn so they have time to settle in before they start flowering, which is usually in summer. Biennials can be planted in autumn to flower the following spring (wallflowers) or in early spring to flower in summer (foxgloves). Hardy annuals can be planted in early spring (or autumn for winter-flowering pansies), but half-hardy or tender plants must not be put out until any danger of frost has passed.

Plants that have grown up in a greenhouse or other sheltered environment may need to be hardened off before being planted out. To gradually acclimatize the plants, start by putting them outside on warm days and then leave them out for longer periods of time until they can be left out overnight. As with trees and shrubs, it is important to keep the plants well watered.

Planting bulbs Most bulbs like to be planted with twice their own depth of soil above them. If your soil is very heavy with clay you should reduce this depth, but be careful not to plant the bulbs too shallowly as they may appear above the ground too soon and risk frost damage.

Dig a hole and put a handful of sand at the bottom to assist drainage and prevent the bulb rotting. If you are going to plant a lot of bulbs it is worth buying a special bulb planter, which will remove a neat plug of soil that you can then replace above the bulb without disturbing the surrounding area. This is particularly useful if you are inserting bulbs into a bed or container that is already fairly full of other plants. It is usually very obvious which way up bulbs should be planted, but this is not always the case with corms (crocus and gladioli). If in doubt lay the corm on its side, as this will cause less damage than planting it upside down.

WATERING, MULCHING AND FEEDING

Watering An adequate supply of water is essential for plants, and in a small garden you will almost certainly need to provide it yourself on a regular basis. Plants within 60cm/24in of a wall and those in containers are particularly at risk, as the wall may create a rain shadow and containers are unable to store a reservoir of water. In a tiny space one or other of these situations will probably affect most of your plants, so you will need to take watering into account when laying out your garden. Roof gardens and balconies that are exposed to the sun and wind tend to dry out quickly and in these areas it is often worth installing an irrigation system, which will either drip water on to the roots or spray the whole plant. Both types of system are effective, but the drip method is more economical in terms of water as less is lost through evaporation.

Water in the evening if you can and use a watering can or the gentle spray on a hose. Blasting plants with a single jet of water can damage them and will wash soil away from the roots. Annuals, containers and especially hanging baskets will need watering once or twice a day during summer, depending on how much they are exposed to sun and wind. Trees and shrubs tend to do better with a good soaking once a week, which will encourage them to grow strong, deeper roots rather than a network of vulnerable surface ones.

Container plants need considerably more water than the equivalent plants growing directly in the soil. The soil in terracotta containers dries out particularly fast as the water is absorbed by the pot as well as evaporating from the soil surface. Water-retaining polymer gels can be useful as they

absorb water and then slowly release it, but you will still need to remember to water – just not as often.

You will probably need to give trees and shrubs in containers a little water throughout the winter. Most plants do not grow much during the cold months, but they will die if they dry out completely. Do not water when the ground is frozen and be careful not to overwater, as much less is lost through evaporation in winter than in summer. Many plants of Mediterranean origin suffer more from damp than frost during the cold months.

You should always try to water plants before they dry out and wilt. A good way to test whether you need to water is to push your finger 5cm/2in down into the soil. It should feel damp, midway between dry and dusty and soggy and waterlogged. Water if the soil is dry.

If the plant is in a container check how fast water drains out of the bottom. If it falls straight through the plant is either too dry or pot bound. To deal with a plant that is too dry, submerge it in a bucket of water and wait until the air bubbles stop rising. This may take up to half an hour if the plant is very dry.

A pot-bound plant has run out of soil and will need to be re-potted in fresh compost in a slightly larger pot, according to the instructions in 'Care of containers' (page 99). Tease out the ends of the roots of a pot-bound plant so they will not continue to grow in circles. Do not increase the size of the container too much as this can shock the plant and damage it. About 5cm/2in all round is probably all that is needed.

Mulching Mulching consists of putting a layer of something over the soil between the plants. Depending on the type of mulch you use, it can have a variety of functions, from enriching the soil to suppressing weeds to conserving water. It is as important to mulch in a tiny garden as in a huge one and, on a small scale, mulching is quick and easy. The various types of mulch and their uses are listed below.

Before applying mulch make sure the soil is weed free and damp. To be effective you need to put down a layer 5cm/2in deep, leaving gaps around the plants so that their stems do not rot. The best times to apply mulch are when planting and thereafter in spring and autumn.

Bark This is a useful and attractive mulch that will prevent weeds and evaporation and deter slugs and snails. It has little nutritional value and breaks down slowly, but will eventually improve the structure of the soil. Composted bark is available at most garden centres and is often the best sort of bark mulch for a tiny garden as the pieces are smaller and fit more easily around little plants. It also has the advantage of breaking down more quickly.

Compost This can be compost you have made yourself (see page 136), mushroom compost, farm manure or a bagged mix bought from a garden centre. Do not confuse it with potting compost, which comes in similar bags but is for planting rather than enriching the soil. Compost should be well rotted before you apply it; you can tell if it is ready as it will be damp and crumbly and have a pleasant earthy smell. A foul-smelling sludge will do more harm than good. Compost is usually neutral, but mushroom compost is alkaline so do not use it around lime-hating plants.

Cocoa shells These are a by-product of the chocolate industry and make a good mulch as they deter slugs and snails, prevent weeds and eventually break down and enrich the soil. The disadvantages are that they can be hard to obtain and, being very light, are only stable when damp.

Grit/pebbles Grit and pebbles have no nutritional value, but they will prevent evaporation and deter slugs and snails. They can also look very attractive, but you must put down a layer thick enough that the soil does not work its way through. This is the best choice for alpines, pinks and other sun-loving plants that do not like rich soil.

Other mulches Alternative mulches you can use are leaf mould, seaweed, straw or a thin layer of grass cuttings. All will break down and enrich the soil, but do not look particularly appealing and are not usually easy to obtain in small quantities.

Feeding As a rough guideline, bought potting compost only has enough nutrients to support a plant for two months. There is a huge variety of plant food available, and the important thing is to give the correct amount of the correct supplement at the correct time. Too much food can do far more harm than too little.

The three main nutrients plants need are nitrogen (N), phosphorus (P) and potassium or potash (K). They also require small amounts of other nutrients, such as calcium, iron and zinc. Very roughly, nitrogen encourages leaf and stem growth, phosphorus is important for root development, especially in young plants, and potassium helps the plant produce flowers and fruit. You are unlikely to need to worry about any of these individually as they are usually present in the soil and general-purpose ready-made foods contain all of them. Bonemeal is good to add at planting as it is high in phosphates, and tomato food will promote both fruit and flowers because it contains potassium. In a small garden, give a supplement such as bonemeal when planting, a general feed in spring to promote growth and tomato food throughout the summer (usually every two weeks) to get the best flowers.

You can provide your plants with food in different ways. Home-made fertilizer is an ideal slow-release food and it is possible to produce compost even in a very limited space (see below). Ready-made products are available as liquid, solid or foliar feed, and can be synthetically made or produced from naturally occurring minerals. They are usually fast acting, and are very handy in a small space as they are easy to store and can be applied as necessary. Foliar feed is the fastest acting and is most useful for plants that have become too weak to take in nutrients via their roots. Slow-release pellets or tablets will let nutrients pass into the soil over a given period of time. With all foods, always follow the instructions and apply when the soil is damp. Try to provide food for your plants before they become starved. Annuals in particular should be fed regularly (every one or two weeks) if you want them to flower throughout summer.

If a plant does not seem to be doing well even after you have provided it with sufficient food and water, it may be suffering from a deficiency of the minerals described above. If you think this is a possibility take a leaf and piece of stem to a local nursery or garden centre. They will know the characteristics of the local soil and should be able to advise you.

COMPOSTING

Even if you only have a balcony you can still make your own compost if you want to. You need no more space than a dustbin would take up and many purpose-made compost bins are attractively designed; some, for example, are disguised as bee hives. Worm bins can be hard to get going, but once established they take up very little space and are extremely efficient at producing really lovely compost. Wormeries with trays are easy to manage as you simply lift out the tray of finished compost and do not have to worry about disturbing the worms.

For the best results compost should be built up in alternate layers of soft and dry material. In a small plastic bin, layers of 5cm/2in are about right. The soft layer can consist of any fruit or vegetable waste, green prunings, coffee grounds and a little grass. The dry layer can be cut-up twigs, straw, dead leaves, eggshells or scrunched newspapers. Avoid adding meat, fish, pet waste from carnivorous animals, diseased plants or perennial weeds.

Turning the compost aerates it and helps it to decompose, but is not vital. Compost activators will speed the process up for you, and are available at garden centres. As you build up your compost you will be able to see how it is developing and add more ingredients accordingly. It will probably take between six and twelve months for the compost to mature, and the end product should be dark and crumbly with a pleasant woodland smell. If some parts are too dry or wet, simply put it back into the bin and recompost until it reaches the right consistency.

PRUNING, TRAINING AND WEEDING

Pruning Most plants do not need pruning in order to survive, although many will remain more vigorous and produce more flowers if cut back regularly. It is a good idea to thin shrubs so that air can circulate through the plant, as this will reduce the risk of disease. Pruning can also be used to keep shrubs to a manageable size or train them into a particular shape.

As a general rule, prune a plant after it has flowered. Most should be left unpruned for a couple of years after planting so they can settle in. Buddleja and lavatera are an exception to this rule as they will grow too large if you don't prune right from the start. Lavender should also be trimmed in the first year as old wood will not grow again.

Always go back to a join or bud (or ground level), and make a clean cut. If you cut back to a bud the new stem will grow out in the direction of the bud. If you want the plant to open up and not become congested, cut back to an outward-facing bud.

Spring-flowering deciduous shrubs These shrubs flower on old wood so do not cut away more than you need to. Remove any dead or weak growth and trim the plant if it is getting leggy. You can cut one or two stems back to ground level to open up the plant, but remember that the new stems will not flower for the first couple of years.

Summer-flowering deciduous shrubs These mostly flower on the current season's growth so you should cut them back hard in spring to encourage lots of new stems. Fast-growing shrubs, such as buddleja and lavatera, should be cut down to a couple of buds above ground level as this will restrict their size as well as increasing the number of flowers. Some shrubs may need cutting again in summer to control their size, but try to avoid cutting off too much as you will be reducing the number of flowering shoots. Dogwoods should be cut back in the spring so lots of bright, new shoots are established by winter.

Broad-leaved evergreens These should not need much pruning. Dead or weak stems should be removed in spring after any risk of frost has passed. At this time you can also shorten any stems if necessary. Avoid cutting back in summer as the plant will be susceptible to winter damage. As evergreens keep their leaves during winter they are more at risk from frost damage than deciduous plants which 'close down' during the cold period.

Conifers These should be pruned in late summer or early autumn. If you prune in spring when they are putting out new growth the cuts will bleed sap, which will weaken the plant. Most conifers should not need much pruning other than to remove dead stems. Apart from yew, conifer branches which are cut from old wood will not re-grow.

Clematis Clematis can be divided into three pruning groups according to when they flower. Even if you do mistakenly cut off too much one year you are unlikely to do the plant any permanent damage.

Spring-flowering clematis do not need pruning and should only be cut back if you need to reduce their size. If necessary cut them back to 30cm/12in above ground after flowering, but the plant may take up to three years to recover and start flowering again. This group includes the smaller-flowered varieties, such as *C. alpina*, *C. armandii*, *C. cirrhosa*, *C, macropetala* and *C. montana*.

Large-flowered clematis that flower early in the summer also do not need much pruning. You can cut them back early in the spring, but each bud you cut off will mean a lost flower as this group flowers on the previous year's growth. The best method is to cut back one-third of the stems to 30cm/12in each year, so you can keep the size of the plant under control without losing too many flowers. This method will also ensure that you get flowers up and down the stems, rather than just at the top.

The late-flowering clematis include both large-flowered varieties and those with smaller flowers such as *C. viticella* and *C. tangutica*. In early spring they should be cut back to 30–60cm/12–24in above ground, and all the old top growth should be removed. These plants flower on the current season's growth so you will get flowers right from the base.

Roses Contrary to popular belief roses are easy to prune and will probably flower regardless of what you do to them. Stems over three years old tend to be less productive and should be cut back to a bud some time between late autumn and early spring. A new stem will grow from the bud so make sure that you cut back to one facing the right direction. This method can be applied to bush and climbing roses. Ramblers flower on old wood so if you want to reduce the size of the plant you should cut one-third of the stems down to the base in summer after flowering. This will control the size without losing too many flowers. All repeat-flowering varieties should be deadheaded as and when the blooms fade. For roses with attractive hips, leave the flower-heads on in autumn.

Wisteria Some wisteria can be hard to get to flower even if you prune them correctly, while others will flower regardless of what you do. It usually pays to be patient as wisterias often take several years to settle in and establish themselves. In mid-summer, after flowering, cut all new growth back to 15cm/6in. You may need to trim the new growth again in the summer if it gets out of control. In mid-winter prune again, cutting the new growth back to two or three buds.

Deadheading This is a very important task in a small garden as you will only have a limited number of plants and deadheading will encourage them to continue flowering for longer than they would naturally. The aim of a great many flowering plants, particularly annuals, is to produce seeds to provide new plants. If you prevent them from doing this by cutting off the fading flowers they will often produce more flowers. Many annuals will go on flowering up until the first frost. Cut the flower neatly back to the next bud or to where it joins the main stem. If you want to collect seeds from the plant, leave some flowers to develop fully towards the end of the summer. Flowers with beautiful seed-heads such as honesty (*Lunaria annua*) and roses with attractive hips should also not be deadheaded at this time.

Training A good space-saving way to keep shrubs under control in a tiny garden is to train them against a wall or fence. Many shrubs other than climbers can be trained in this way, as long as you are vigilant about pruning and tying in. Fruit trees will particularly benefit from this treatment, as they will be protected from the wind and warmed by the wall.

Before planting anything you need to put up a framework to tie the plant to. You can use trellis or galvanized wire depending on whether or not you want the support to show. Attach trellis to wooden spacers nailed to the wall or fence, which will give you a uniform space for tying plants (see page 126 for more on trellis). Use vine eyes to keep wires away from a wall and allow you to tighten the wire if necessary.

When you first plant a climber, spread out its branches and fix them loosely to the support with ties or garden twine, leaving space for the stems to grow. Plants tend to grow upwards so if you want the whole wall covered spread out some stems almost horizontally from the base. As more shoots develop over the seasons spread them to fill the gaps, again tying in place. Do this regularly as new growth develops. Prune the plant at the same time as you would normally, but also prune to cut away unwanted growth and to encourage new growth by cutting back to a bud that is facing in a suitable direction.

You can train plants into a variety of shapes but you must make sure they grow as you want them to right from the start. Fans are trained and pruned so that all the branches extend from a single point near the base. Spread out the stems in a semicircle and try to ensure equal growth all round, moving stems a little if necessary as they grow. If you are training a plant such as blackberry, which to fruit well needs its alternate stems cut right back every other year, prune the plant so you cut back alternate arms of the fan each year. Many plants can be easily trained into a fan, but the following adapt especially well: *Ceanothus*, flowering quince (*Chaenomeles*), cotoneaster (*Cotoneaster horizontalis*), forsythia (*Forsythia suspensa*), pyracantha, flowering currant, fig and fruit trees that bear stoned fruit, such as plum and peach.

An espalier has a single vertical stem from which horizontal branches grow outwards. Choose a strong, straight stem as the upright and fix this vertically to the trellis. All the other stems must be trained horizontally from this one, ideally at equal distances apart. Trim away any unwanted growth and tie all the other stems in place. If you do this while they are young the stems will adjust happily. Small shoots will grow up along each horizontal stem, providing interest along the whole length. The overall effect should be very neat and formal and is particularly suited to apples, pears and wisteria.

Weeding Weeds are either annuals, which can be dealt with easily, or perennials, which can be more of a problem but are still possible to clear in a small space. A 5cm/2in layer of mulch should deter most weed seeds. If you only have containers filled with bagged potting compost, weeds should not be a problem at all as the compost should not contain any perennial weeds and any annuals that grow up can be removed as they appear.

Annual weeds are easy to pull up when young and can be composted as long as they have not set seed. Dealing with annual weeds before they set seed will save a lot of work in subsequent years. A single plant of fat hen (*Chenopodium album*) can produce 70,000 seeds, which is an awful lot of weeds for a small garden. Hoeing is the traditional method of getting rid of weeds, but in a tiny garden it is much easier to pull them up by hand. Be careful not to pull up small seedlings as many plants look remarkably similar when young.

Perennial weeds can be a much more serious problem and in a small space it is really worth trying to get rid of them before you start planting. Bindweed, horsetail, ground elder and couch grass will all take over your garden if given half a chance, and even a tiny piece of root left in the soil will re-grow into a monster plant. Clear the soil really thoroughly by digging it over and removing all the roots. Then leave for a couple of weeks so you can pull up any shoots that appear. Bindweed spreads via seeds as well as roots, so you must be vigilant about removing new plants.

DEALING WITH PESTS AND DISEASES

The unnaturally confined environment of a garden makes all the plants grown there susceptible to pests and diseases, but there are certain steps you can take to avoid this becoming a problem. Always buy healthy plants, as they will be better able to resist predators and disease. Put plants in good soil, give them the correct amount of sun or shade, and take care that air can circulate around the plants. Try to plant disease-resistant varieties; *Clematis viticella*, for example, is immune to clematis wilt, which can destroy a seemingly healthy plant overnight. Always clear away piles of fallen leaves or rubbish as these can encourage pests and diseases.

Keep an eye out for anything that looks unhealthy and get to know how your plants should look so you can spot any potential problems early on. In a small garden, pests and diseases can be dealt with fairly easily. Remember that a plant that does not seem to be doing well may simply be suffering from insufficient watering or feeding (see pages 135 and 136).

Pests All gardens will be affected by some pests and it is no use trying to get rid of all of them. You will be waging a constant war against nature. A much easier approach is simply to encourage the pests to go somewhere else. Most will not do the garden lasting harm and those that do cause great damage, such as the bright red lily beetles, can be picked off and destroyed as soon as they appear.

Pesticides may seem to provide an easy solution for dealing with pests, but they upset the garden's ecological balance and will undoubtedly cause long-term damage. Biological controls can be used safely and effectively against most pests. These mimic the controls that occur naturally in the wild, but in increased intensity to deal with the greater density of plants in your garden. Organic insecticides based on rotenone or pyrethrins are also safe and widely available.

Slugs and snails These are the bane of all gardeners everywhere. Snails live in brickwork and slugs live in soil, so the character of your garden will determine which you have. If you are unlucky you will have both.

Pesticides are not much use against slugs and snails; tests have found that slug pellets only reduce the population by 10 per cent. Throwing them over the garden wall does not help much either, as it was found that marked snails simply slimed their way back to their original garden. Buckets of salt water will kill slugs and snails and beer left out overnight will attract and drown them. The snag with these methods is that you are still left with the revolting corpses to deal with.

Entire books have been written on how to deal with slugs and snails, but a much easier approach is simply to deter them in the first place. Many plants are not affected anyway, and the vulnerable ones can be protected by a ring that the slugs and snails will not cross. Sharp gravel is very effective and looks attractive. Simply sprinkle a 2.5cm/1in ring around the plant. Eggshells also work, but are unsightly. Mats and collars for individual plants are available, and you can protect containers by fixing copper tape around the top. This looks quite appealing and although it is expensive it lasts well and is 100 per cent effective. Make sure no leaves overhang the barrier as slugs or snails will use them as an edible ladder. New growth is particularly vulnerable, so it is best to keep young plants in a protected place and plant them out when they are larger and too tough to be eaten.

Slugs and snails have many natural enemies and if you encourage birds, frogs, toads and hedgehogs into your garden they will eat them for you. If your garden is too small to attract enough predators you can use biological controls. Nematodes are natural parasites that kill slugs and small

snails. They are mixed with water and applied to the soil every 6–8 weeks.

Plants vulnerable to slugs/snails
Clematis
Delphiniums
Hostas
Lupins
Marigolds (*Calendula* and *Tagetes*)
Stocks (*Matthiola*)
Tobacco plants (*Nicotiana*)
Tulips
Most seedlings and young plants
Many vegetables

Plants resistant to slugs/snails
Spiky or hairy plants
Most herbs
Anything with tough, leathery leaves

Aphids (greenfly) Aphids are another pest high on every gardener's hit list. They stunt growth, distort leaves and can increase the risk of viruses and mould. It is easier to prevent the problem than to try to cure it. Garlic has traditionally been planted by roses to deter greenfly, and this trick works for almost all plants. Avoid using garlic from supermarkets as it is sometimes treated to stop it growing. Simply plant a clove in each container and beside any vulnerable plants. The leaves will be unobtrusive and the smell of garlic will not be transmitted to the plant you are protecting. Other plants which aphids dislike are onions, garlic, spearmint (*Mentha spicata*), poached egg plant (*Limnanthes douglasii*) and lavender.

In a small space, it is possible to remove any aphids that do appear by brushing them off with your fingers. A strong jet of water will also get rid of them, as will a spray with a weak soapy solution, but neither of these options is particularly satisfactory on small, delicate buds. A weak solution of seaweed spray should deter the aphids and will benefit rather than harm the plant. Birds, ladybirds and lacewings all eat aphids, but are unlikely to clear them from your garden as they breed so fast. Nematodes are a biological control that will help without upsetting the natural balance of the garden.

Ants These can be a problem as they 'farm' aphids for the sticky honeydew the aphids excrete. If you get rid of the aphids the ants should go elsewhere. Ants' nests can be destroyed by pouring boiling water on them.

Caterpillars Caterpillars eat a huge amount, but they do turn into beautiful butterflies. The easiest approach is to pick the caterpillars gently off the plants and throw them over the fence, hoping that they eat and grow elsewhere and return to your garden as a butterfly. This is not a particularly neighbourly method, but if your neighbours are not as vigilant as you then that is their problem! Basil, borage, hyssop, rosemary, sage and thyme will all deter the cabbage white caterpillar, which is often the worst offender.

Vine weevil If a plant is looking generally unwell it is possible that vine weevil grubs are eating the roots. The matt black beetles lay up to 1500 eggs each every summer and the grubs then spend the winter eating your plants. Vines, camellias, heucheras and all container plants are at risk. Between spring and autumn the adults can be killed by applying nematodes in water, or you can put barrier glue around the containers to stop the adults climbing in.

Shield bug The brown shield bug causes little harm to gardens, but the bright-green bug, which thrives in warm conditions, can potentially be a great problem as it eats a variety of vegetables and fruit, particularly soft fruit. On all plants it increases the risk of disease. The bugs are easy to spot and should be picked off and destroyed.

Other pests Cats, squirrels and birds are the only other pests you are likely to encounter in a small garden. Cats can be deterred from using your garden as a litter tray by a sharp jet from the hose, which will do them no harm. Squirrels may look entertaining and can seem quite friendly, but beware of encouraging them as they will bury nuts in your flowerbeds and dig up your bulbs in autumn. If a jet of water does not discourage them a sharp tap on the bottom with a garden cane will. This will not injure the animal but should put it off coming into your garden. On the whole birds do more good than harm by eating predators. If you are growing seeds in an open bed, cover it with netting for safety. You can also protect fruit trees from birds with netting.

Diseases Plant diseases can be present in the soil, carried in the air or spread by insects. Strong, healthy plants will be able to withstand most diseases so, again, it is better to aim for prevention rather than cure. Keep your plants as happy as possible and allow air to circulate around them to avoid fungal growth. Make sure your soil drains correctly, neither too fast nor too slow. Damping off is a problem that often affects seedlings if they get too moist. To avoid it, sow the seedlings thinly and do not overwater. If they do start to droop and die there is little you can do other than thin them, cut down the water and learn for next time.

Below is a list of the diseases you are most likely to encounter and an explanation of how to deal with them without using chemicals.

Botrytis (grey mould)
Furry grey mould appears on the leaves and faded flowers. This is caused by damp conditions so you should increase the air circulation by pruning, and reduce the amount of water.

Canker
Dead and wrinkled stems appear. Cut away affected branches and destroy them. Ensure the plant is in suitable conditions so it can fight future infections. In fruit trees bad drainage is usually a contributing factor.

Coral spot
Orange or pink fungus appears. Cut away the diseased parts and destroy them. Make sure the plant is as healthy as possible by keeping it in its preferred conditions.

Honey fungus
Black strands grow up the stems. The plant weakens and eventually dies. This is serious. You must remove all traces of the plant, destroying it completely. Plant a resistant variety in the space left.

Leaf curl
The leaves curl up and drop early. Remove affected leaves and spray new growth with a weak seaweed solution.

Powdery mildew
White powder appears on the leaves and stems. This is caused by dryness. Water well and mulch to conserve the dampness. It is often possible to buy resistant varieties.

Rust
Orange patches appear on the leaves. This is caused by too much nitrogen and will weaken the plant if left unattended. Remove the affected leaves and spray the remaining ones with a weak seaweed solution.

Viruses
A great variety of viruses are spread by flying insects or in the soil. The symptoms vary according to the virus and can include weak or stunted growth, poor development of fruit and marks on the leaves or flowers. Once affected most plants need to be dug up and destroyed. The risk of viruses can be greatly reduced by destroying aphids and keeping your plants in good condition. If you are growing vegetables you should rotate their positions so the soil does not become exhausted and infected.

Index

Page numbers in *italic* refer to the captions to the illustrations. Vegetables, fruit and herbs are included in the index under their common names.

Abutilon 72
　megapotamicum 126
Acaena 96
Acanthus spinosus 66, 122
access 16, 32, 36, 52
Acer 59, 69, *75*, 77, 78
　japonicum 86
　palmatum 82, 86
Aconitum 77
Actinidia kolomikta 66, 71, 126
Adiantum 31
Aeonium 'Zwartkop' 122
Agapanthus 59, 122
Agave 29, *43*, *48*, 59, *127*
　americana 82
　　'Marginata' 122
　parviflora 122
Ajuga reptans 93
Akebia quinata 32, 53, 66, *84*, 126
Alcea rosea (hollyhocks) 18, 76
Alchemilla mollis 59, 85, 93
Allium 76, 77
　cristophii 29, 122
Aloysia triphylla 88
alpines 94, 98, 99
Amelanchier 77
　canadensis 82, 86
　x *grandiflora* 82
Anemone 18, 63
　blanda 76
　hupehensis 41, 66, 76, 77
　x *hybrida* 41, 66, 76, 77, 89
annuals
　deadheading 137–8
　growing 87–8, 134–5, 136
ants 139
aphids 107, 139
Aponogeton 113
apple trees 104, *106*
apricots 104
Aquilegia 63, 76
Arabis caucasia 93
arbours 45, *65*, 66
Arbutus 48
arches, trellis 32
architectural plants 117, 122
Argyranthemum 76, *98*
Armeria (thrift) 59, 93, *95*
Artemisia
　absinthium 'Lambrook Silver' 18, 23
　'Powis Castle' 18
Aruncus dioicus 65
Arundinaria 36

Arundo donax 57, 59
Asplenium scolopendrium 36
　Cristatum Group 36
Astelia chathamica 24, *110*
Aster 77
Astrantia 63
Athyrium filix-femina 62
Aubrieta 76, 93
Aucuba japonica
　'Crotonifolia' 63
autumn interest *75*, 77–8
awnings 45, 50
Azara microphylla 86, 88
Azolla filiculoides 112

balconies 42–5, *43*–*5*, *47*, 57
　surveys 8, 42
bamboo *45*, *65*, *84*, 85, 87, *98*
　see also individual species
bark *47*, 135
basements 36–41, *39*–*40*, *116*
basil 104
bay trees 85, 86, 102, 104
beetroot 107
Begonia 101
Berberis 27, 59, 69, 76, 78
　thunbergii 'Rose Glow' 63
　wilsoniae 77
bergamot 76, 104
Bergenia 18, 93
　cordifolia 77
Betula
　pendula 'Youngii' 86
　utilis var. *jacquemontii 23*
biennials 88, 134–5
biological controls 139
blackberries 106, 138
blackcurrants 106
bluebells 76, 88
borage 104
botrytis 140
Bougainvillea 126
boundaries 8–9, *21*, 66, 124–9
　roofs 47
box *see Buxus*
Brachyscome 101
brassicas 107
bricks 23
Briza maxima 87
brooms 133
Brunnera macrophylla 77, 93
Buddleja 57, 59, 69, 137
　davidii 76
bulbs 27, 76, 77, 88–9
　planting 135
busy Lizzie 36, 41, 45, 63, 77, 100
Buxus 27, 60, *129*
　sempervirens 32, *40*, 59, 76

'Suffruticosa' *91*
buying plants 132

cacti *48*
Callicarpa bodinieri var. *giraldii* 77, 78
Callitriche hermaphroditica 112
Calluna vulgaris 76
　see also heathers
Caltha palustris 112
Camellia 68, 69, 71, 72
Campanula
　carpatica 31, 93
　cochleariifolia 31, 93
　portenschlagiana 31, 93
　poscharskyana 31, 93, 101
Campsis radicans 69, 72, 126
candles 27, 116, *118*
canker 140
capsicums 107
Carex 77
　elata 'Aurea' 122
　oshimensis 'Evergold' 63
carrots 107
Caryopteris 59
caterpillars 139–40
Ceanothus 72, 76, 138
　arboreus 'Trewithen Blue' 66
　'Autumnal Blue' 66
　gloriosus 93
　hearstiorum 93
Centaurea 59
Centranthus ruber 59
Ceratostigma 69, 76, 77
Cercis siliquastrum 69, 76, 86
Chaenomeles 71, 72, 76, 138
　speciosa 32
chamomile 92, 104, *106*
cherry trees 104
chervil 104
children's play areas 11
chillies 107
Chimonanthus praecox 72, 77, 78
chives 102, 104, *106*, 107
Choisya 27, 36, *47*, 59, 72, 76
　ternata 'Sundance' 16, *40*, 60–61, 63
Chusquea culeou 87
Cistus 29, 59, 72
Citrus
　limon 82, 86, 94, 104, *109*
　sinensis 82, 86, *86*, 94, 104
Clematis 32, *50*, 52, 69, 71, 126
　pruning 137

alpina 66
　armandii 66
　'Bill MacKenzie' *77*
　cirrhosa 66
　macropetala 66, 72
　montana 66
　tangutica 77
　viticella 36, 77, 126, 138
climbers 32–4, 57, 71–2, 126, 129
　stairs 52–3
　training 18, 66, 138
clover 92
Cobaea scandens 126
cocoa shells 136
Colchicum speciosum 77
　'Album' 77
colour 32, *116*
　boundaries 8–9, 36, *39*, 124
　plants 36, 53, *75*, 76–8, 82
companion planting 102, 107
compost 135–6
　potting 98, 136
　roof gardens 50
computer programmes 8
concrete 23
conifers, pruning 137
containers 94–101
　balconies 42, 45
　passages 11, 34
　patios 27
　planting and care 98–100, 132, 135
　roof gardens 50
　steps 52–3, *53*
　trees 85, 86, 99
　vegetables 107
　walls *72*, 126, *127*
　for winter 78
Convolvulus
　cneorum 18
　sabatius 101
coral spot 140
cordons 106, *106*
Cordyline 45
　australis 82, 122
coriander 104
Cornus 59
　alba 'Sibirica' *57*
Cosmos
　atrosanguineus 88
　bipinnatus 77
Cotoneaster 72, 78
　dammeri 93
　horizontalis 77, 138
courgettes 107
Crataegus 59, 76, 86
　laevigata 'Paul's Scarlet' 68
Crocosmia 77
Crocus 59, 76
　banaticus 77
　cartwrightianus 77

sieberi 77
　subsp. *sublimis*
　　'Tricolor' 78
cucumber 107
cutting flowers 89
Cycas 39
Cyclamen 39
　hederifolium 77
Cymbalaria muralis 40
Cynara cardunculus 122
Cytisus 59, 69
　battandieri 88

Dahlia 89
　'Bishop of Llandaff' *58*
Daphne 77
　bholua 'Jaqueline Postill' 78
　odora 18
　　'Aureomarginata' 16, 18
dark areas *see* shade
Darmera peltata 63
Dasylirion acrotrichum 96
deadheading 132, 137–8
decking *24*, 26, *47*, *113*, *116*
design process 8–13
Dianthus 59, 76, 88
　barbatus 88
Diascia 101
Dicentra spectabilis 41, 76
Dicksonia antarctica 39, *45*, 82
Dieffenbachia 39
Digitalis, (foxglove) 18, 60, 63, 66, 76
dill 104
diseases 140
drainage
　roof gardens 48
　soil 133
drought-tolerant plants 59
dwarf beans 107

east-facing walls 71, 72
eating outside *13*, 27, 34
Eccremocarpus scaber 72, 126
Echeveria 127
Echinacea purpurea 'White Swan' *102*
Eichhornia crassipes 112
Eleagnus 16, 42
　x *ebbingei* 'Gilt Edge' 63
equipment 132–3
Eranthis 59, 63, 77
Erica 93
　see also heathers
Erigeron karvinskianus 93
Eryngium 59, 122
Erysimum cheiri (wallflowers) 27, 59, 76, 88
Escallonia 42, *47*, 66, 69, 72, 76

Eschscholzia californica 59, 77
espaliers 31, *82*, 104, 138
Euonymus 32, 59, 60
　fortunei 57, 72
　　'Silver Queen' 63
Euphorbia 48, 60
　characias subsp. *wulfenii* 122
exposure 9–10, 47, 57–9

Fagus sylvatica 'Purpurea Pendula' 85, 86
fans 104, 138
Fargesia
　murieliae 122
　nitida 122
Fatsia japonica 36, 41, 122
feeding 134, 136
fences *21*, 32, 126
fennel *106*
ferns 57, 60, 71, 72, *110*, *123*
　see also individual species
fertilizers 134, 136
Festuca glauca 76, 93, 122
feverfew *106*
Ficus (fig) 59, 104–6, 138
fish 110
flowerbeds 26, 30–31
　see also soil
focal points 11, 66, 82, 114, 117
Forsythia 69, 71, 72, 76
　suspensa 63, 72, 138
fountains 31, *34*, 109, *113*
foxgloves *see Digitalis*
fragrance 18, 31, 41, 88, 89
French beans 107
Fritillaria
　imperialis 122
　meleagris 17
　　var. *unicolor* subvar. *alba* 17
front gardens 16–21
frost 71, 104
fruit bushes 102, 106
fruit trees 71, 72, 82, 86, 104–6
　training 104, 138
Fuchsia 42, *50*, 59, 63, 76
　containers 27, 36, 101
furniture *13*, 115, *116*
　choosing 27

Galanthus (snowdrops) 60, 76, 77, 78
garlic 104, 107, 139
Garrya elliptica 72
Gaura lindheimeri 77
Genista 59, 76
Geranium 59, 63, 76, 93
　macrorrhizum 93
Gladiolus 77, 89
Glechoma hederacea
　'Variegata' 101, *106*
globe artichokes *102*

gooseberries 106
gourds 107
granite setts 23
grape vines *see Vitis*
grasses 85, 87, 94, *95*, 100
gravel 23, 36, 47, 93
greenfly 107, 139
greenhouses 115
grey mould 140
grit 136
ground cover plants 93, *93*
Gypsophila repens 93

Hamamelis 88
　japonica 'Zucchariniana' *89*
hand tools 132–3
hanging baskets 18, 101, 135
heathers 45, 52, 76, 78, 93, *93*
Hebe 42, 59, 69, 76
　x *franciscana* 'Variegata' 63
　'Great Orme' 18
　pinguifolia 'Pagei' 93
Hedera (ivy) 36, 93, *125*
　shade tolerance 32, 52, 63, 66, 126
　topiary 16
　wind tolerance 42, 59
　canariensis 'Gloire de Morengo' 41
　helix 101
　　'Adam' 60
　　'Angulus Aurea' 41
　　'Buttercup' 41
　　'Glacier' 60
　　'Oro di Bogliasco' ('Goldheart') 60
hedges 16, 47, 66, 124
Helianthemum 93
Helianthus annuus 18, 77, 122
Helichrysum 45
　petiolare 45, 101
Helleborus 18, 63, 77
　foetidus 62
　x *hybridus* 41
　niger 41, 78
　orientalis 78
herbs 71, 88, 102–4, *105*
　shade tolerance 61, 104
　window boxes 31, 100, 102
Hesperis matronalis 18, 76, 88
Hibiscus 69
holly *see Ilex*
hollyhocks 18, 76
honey fungus 140
honeysuckle *see Lonicera*
Hordeum jubatum 85, 87
Hosta 41, 60, *61*, 63, 93, *123*
　crispula 63
　sieboldiana var. *elegans* 122
Hottonia palustris 112
Humulus lupulus 'Aureus' 32,

72, 126
Hyacinthoides non-scripta (bluebells) 76, 88
Hydrangea 31, *39*, *69*, 72, 76, *100*
　shade tolerance 61, *63*
　anomala subsp, *petiolaris* 66
　macrophylla 10
Hydrocharis morsus-ranae 112, 113

Ilex 86
　aquifolium 36, 59, 68, 69, 76, 77, 122
　　'Silver Queen' 63
illusions 11, *34*, 47, 115, 124, 126
　trompe l'oeil 115, 117, *123*, 124
　see also mirrors
Impatiens (busy Lizzie) 36, 41, 45, 63, 77, 100
insecticides 139
Ipomoea (morning glory) 18, 66, 71, 72, 77, 126
Iris
　laevigata 112
　pallida 'Variegata' 93
　pseudacorus 112
　unguicularis 77
　versicolor 112
irrigation systems 48, 135
ivy *see Hedera*

Jasminum
　nudiflorum 34, 52, 71, 72, 77, 126
　officinale 18, 27, 53, 66, 72, 76, 126
　x *stephanense* 18, 27, 53, 66, 126
Juncus f. *effusus* 'Spiralis' 112
Juniperus
　horizontalis 93
　procumbens 93
　scopulorum 'Skyrocket' 86, 122

Kerria japonica 'Pleniflora' 63, 76
kitchen gardens 31, 102–7
Kniphofia 77, 122

Laburnum 65
Lagarosiphon major 112
Lagerstroemia indica 86
Lamium maculatum 41, 57, 60, 93
　'Beacon Silver' *93*
Lathyrus
　latifolius 59, 66, 72, 126
　odoratus (sweet pea) 18, 77, 87, 88, *102*, 126
Laurus nobilis (bay) 85, 86, 102, 104
Lavandula *50*, 76, 82, 88, 137

dry conditions 48, 57, 59
　angustifolia 18, *31*
　stoechas 18, *106*
Lavatera 76, 137
lawns 91–2, *91*
leaf curl 140
legal restrictions 8
lemon balm *106*
lemon trees 82, 86, 94, 104, *109*
Leptospermum 72
lettuce *106*, 107
Leucojum vernum 77
light wells 36–41, *39*–*40*
lighting 27, 36, *39*, 50, *53*, 115–16, *118*–*20*
　candles 27, 116, *118*
　spotlights *118*
　and water features 109
Ligularia przewalskii 63
Ligustrum ovalifolium
　'Aureum' 63
Lilium 27, *35*, *61*, 77, 100
　regale 31, 122
lily beetles 139
Lobelia erinus 36, 45, 101
Lobularia maritima 93
loganberries 106
Lonicera 52, 71, 72, 76, 88, 126
　x *americana* 18
　x *heckrottii* 18
　henryi 66
　japonica 66
　nitida 'Baggesen's Gold' 16
　periclymenum 66, *69*
　　'Belgica' 18
　　'Serotina' 18
　tragophylla 66
Lotus hirsutus 48
Lunaria annua 63, 76
Lysimachia nummularia
　'Aurea' 61, 93

Magnolia 69, 72, *75*, 76
　stellata 76, 86
　wilsonii 69
Mahonia 47, 76
　aquifolium 41
　japonica 60
　x *media* 'Charity' 41
maintenance 132–8
　water features 113
Malus (crab apple) 69, 76, 82, 86
　see also apple trees
marigolds 107
marjoram 104
Matthiola
　incana 88
　longipetala subsp. *bicornis* 31
Meconopsis betonicifolia 57
Melianthus major *24*, 122
Menyanthes trifoliata 113
metal gridwork *24*
Mimulus
　cardinalis 101

luteus 61
mint 102, 104
mirrors *24*, 36, *39*, 109, 117, *123*
Miscanthus sinensis 'Kleine Fontane 87, 122
Molinia caerulea 87
Monarda (bergamot) 76, 104
morning glory *see Ipomoea*
mosaics 36
moss 92
mulches 57, 71, 135–6
Myosotis 63, 76
　scorpioides 'Mermaid' 112
Myriophyllum verticillatum 112
Myrrhis 65

Narcissus 17, 59, 76, 77, *77*
　bulbocodium 88
　'Spellbinder' 88
nasturtiums *see Tropaeolum*
Nemophila
　maculata 93
　menziesii 93
Nerine 72
Nerium oleander 45
Nicotiana (tobacco plant) *50*, 77
　for fragrance 18, 31, 88
　shade tolerance 36, 41, 63
　'Lime Green' 61
Nigella damascena 77
noise 18, 109
north-facing walls 71, 72
Nymphaea 113, *113*
Nymphoides peltata 113, *113*

Oenothera biennis 59, 77, 88
Olea europaea (olive) 82, 86, 94, 104, 122
Omphalodes cappadocica 41, 76, 93
onions 107
orange trees 82, 86, *86*, 94, 104
oregano 104
ornaments 116–17, *123*
Ornithogalum thyrsoidea 71
Orontium aquaticum 113
Osmanthus 88
　x *burkwoodii* 16
　delavayi 72
　heterophyllus *40*

Pachysandra terminalis 93
　'Variegata' 63
Papaver 76, 77
　orientale 59
　somniferum 87
parsley 102, *102*, 104
Parthenocissus
　henryana 71, 126
　quinquefolia 18, 66, 71, 72, 77–8, 126
passages 32, *32*, 34, *34*–*5*
Passiflora caerulea (passion flower) 71, 126
patios 23–7

paving 23, *23*, *24*, 36, 47, 92
peaches 104, 138
pear trees *82*, 104
pebbles 136
Pelargonium 34, 101
   containers 27, 45, *53*, *72*, 94
   window boxes *45*, 100, *100*
   'Attar of Roses' 31
   'Copthorne' 31
   'Lady Plymouth' 31, *106*
   'Mabel Grey' 31
   tomentosum 31
Pennisetum 59
peppers 107
perennials 89
   containers 94
   growing 85, 87, 134–5
periwinkle 60, 63
Persicaria affinis 93
pests and diseases 102, 138–40
Petunia 96, 100
   Surfinia Series 101
pH tests 10
Philadelphus 59, 76, 88
   'Manteau d'Hermine' *89*
Phlox paniculata 88
Phormium 57, 59
   cookianum 122
   tenax 66, 76
   'Dazzler' 63, 122
Phyllostachys 29, 36
   aurea 122
   nigra 87
Picea glauca var. *albertiana*
   'Conica' 86
Pieris 63, 76
Pistia stratiotes 112
Pittosporum
   tenuifolium 86
   tobira 58
plans 8, 13
planting 132, 134–5
   climbers 129
   containers 98–100
Pleioblastus viridistriatus 87
plum trees 104, 138
pollution 68–9
Polygonatum 62, 63, *65*
Polypodium 76
Polystichum 31, 76
   setiferum 41
pools 108–110, *109*, *113*
pot-bound plants 135
Potamogeton crispus 112
potatoes 107
Potentilla 48, 59
pots *see* containers
potting compost 98
powdery mildew 140
Primula 63
privacy 9, 16, 66
pruning 57, 102, 136–8
Prunus 69, 72, 86
   cerasus 71
Pulmonaria 36, 63, 76, 77, 78, 93

'Lewis Palmer' 41
   rubra 41
Pyracantha 63, 69
   wall plants 32, 72, 126, 138
   year-round interest 76, 77, 78
Pyrus 69
   calleryana 'Chanticleer' *82*
   salicifolia 'Pendula' 86
   see also pear trees

quinces 104
   see also Chaenomeles

radishes 107
raised beds 11, 18, 26, 60
   construction 30–31, 50
Ranunculus aquatilis 112
raspberries *65*, 106
redcurrants 106
Reseda odorata 88
retaining walls 26–7, 30–31
Ribes 72
rocket 107
roofs 46–50, *48*, *50*, *57*, *105*
   exposure 9, 47, 57–9, 71
   surveys 8, 47
Rosa 50, 69, 76, *129*
   climbers 34, 71, 72, 126
   pruning 57, 137
   'Climbing Iceberg' *78*
   English roses 85
   'Fru Dagmar Hastrup' *89*
   'Gloire de Dijon' 18
   'Maigold' 18
   'New Dawn' 18, *21*
   'Pink Perpetue' 18
   'Queen Mother' 27
   'Zéphirine Drouhin' 18, 27
rosemary 102, 104
   see also Rosmarinus officinalis
Rosmarinus officinalis 16, 48, 57, 59, 69, 82
   'Prostratus' 93
runner beans 106, 107, 126
rust 140

sage *59*, 102, 104, *106*
Salix caprea 'Kilmarnock' 85, 86
Salvia 77
   officinalis 59, 104
   'Icterina' *106*
   'Kew Gold' 102
   'Purpurascens' 102
   'Tricolor' 102
Salvinia auriculata 112
Santolina chamaecyparissus 31, 93
Saponaria ocymoides 93
Sarcococca 69, 72, 77, 88
Sarracenia 29
Saxifragia
   stolonifera 'Tricolor' 93
   x *urbium* 93

Scaevola aemula 101
scented plants 18, 31, 41, 88, 89
Schoenoplectus lacustris
   subsp. *tabernaemontani* 'Zebrinus' *110*
Scilla 76, 77
screens 9, 66
   see also trellis
sculpture *32*, *35*, *43*, *116*, *123*
secateurs 133
Sedum 48, *93*, *96*, *100*
   kamtschaticum 31
   morganianum 122
   spathulifolium 31, 93
   spectabile 77
seeds 134, 138
Semiarundinaria fastuosa 87
Sempervivum 93, *127*
   tectorum 93
shade *32–41*, *35*, *39–40*, 60–63, 71
shelter 41, 42, 57, 124
   roofs 47, *50*
shield bugs 140
shrubs
   choosing 85
   planting 134
   pruning 57, 136–7
site evaluation 8–10
Skimmia 52, 69
   japonica 77, 78
slugs and snails 139
snowdrops 60, 76, 77, 78
soil
   drainage 133
   preparation and improvement 30, 60, 133–4
   roof gardens 50
   types 10
Solanum crispum 72
   'Glasnevin' 126
Soleirolia soleirolii 93
Solomon's seal *62*, 63, *65*
sorrel 107
south-facing walls 71, 72
spinach 107
sprayers 133
spring interest 76
Stachys byzantina 23, 48, 57, 59, 93
stepping stones 91, 93
steps *17*, 36, 52–3, *53*
stone slabs 23
storage 32, 36, 115, *116*
Stratiotes aloides 112, 113
strawberries 106, *106*
summer interest 76–7
sunflowers 18, 77, 122
supports for plants 57, 66, 124, 126, 133, 138
   see also trellis
surface materials 23, *23*, *24*, 26
   roofs 47
surveys 8, 42, 47

Sutera cordata 53, *127*
sweet pea *see Lathyrus odoratus*
sweetcorn *106*
swings *11*
Swiss chard 107
Syringa 76, 88
   meyeri 'Palibin' 18
   pubescens subsp. *patula* 'Miss Kim' 18
   vulgaris 69

Tanacetum 93
   parthenium 'Aurem' *106*
tarragon 102, 104
Taxus baccata 69
   'Fastigiata' 86
   'Standishii' 86
tayberries 106
temperature 50, 124
terracotta pots 97, 135
Teucrium fruticans 93
theft 16
Thunbergia alata 101
thyme 31, 92, 102, 104
Tiarella cordifolia 93
tiles 23, *24*
timber decking *24*, 26, 47
tobacco plants *see Nicotiana*
tomatoes 107
tools 132–3
topiary 16, *18*, *78*, 100, 117, *122*
Trachycarpus fortunei 82
trailing plants 100, 101
training plants 36, 129, 138
trees
   choosing 82, 85, 86
   containers 85, 86, 99
   planting 134
trellis 32, 36, 126–9, *128*
   arbours 45
   screens 9, 42, 57, *58*, 66, *72*, *127*
   for shade 50
Trifolium
   pratense 'Susan Smith' 92
   repens 'Purpurascens Quadrifolium' 92
trompe-l'oeil 115, 117, *123*, 124
Tropaeolum (nasturtium) 36, 45, 66, 77, 101, 126
   speciosum 126
tropical gardens 82, *84*
troughs *see* containers
Tulipa 76
turf 91
Typha minima 112

variegated plants 60–61, 63
vegetables 31, 106–7
Verbena 76, *98*
   bonariensis 18, *31*, *58*, 77, 100
   Tapien Series 101
Viburnum 36, 59, 66, 69, 77
   x *bodnantense* 'Dawn' *78*

tinus 76
   'Eve Price' 18, 66
   'Gwenllian' 66, 78
views 8–9
Vinca 60, 76
   minor 93, 101
   'Variegata' 63
vine weevil 140
vines *see Vitis*
Viola 52, 63
   x *wittrockiana* 77, 78
viruses 139, 140
Vitis 65, 77, 106
   'Brant' 66, 126
   coignetiae 66, 126
   vinifera 126

Waldsteinia ternata 93
wallflowers 27, 59, 76, 88
walls 36, 71–2, 124–6, *125*
   plants for 71–2, 126, 129
water features *24*, 36, 109–113
   see also fountains
water plants 110–113
water supply 48
watering 41, 48, 133, 135
   containers 99, 132
weeding 138
Weigela 76
   florida
      'Foliis Purpureis' 18
      'Variegata' 18
west-facing walls 71, 72
whitefly 107
wildlife 89
wind 9–10, 42, 47, 57–9
wind-tolerant plants 59
window boxes *43*, 100, *100*, 102, *106*
windows 34, 66
winter interest 77, 78
Wisteria 18, 66, 72, 76
   pruning 137
   sinensis 126
wormeries 136

Yucca
   filamentosa 122
   gloriosa 59

Zantedeschia aethiopica 112

Photographic acknowledgments

Nicola Browne: 20 (designer Evan English with Dan Pearson), 29 right (designer Philipe Nash), 38 (designer Jinny Blom), 48 (designer Dan Pearson), 49 (designer Ross Palmer), 56 (design Avant Gardener), 58 (designer Jinny Blom), 87 (designer Evan English), 92 right (designer Ross Palmer), 93 left (design Arends Nursery), 94–5 (designer Dan Pearson), 97 (designer Ross Palmer), 101 (designer Ross Palmer), 110–11 (designer Ross Palmer), 114–15 (designer Ross Palmer), 127 above right (design Avant Gardener)

Caroline Clark: 16 right–17, 18, 21 left, 34 (courtesy of Jean Wild), 40–1, 46, 62 above right, 62 below right, 67, 74, 76 left, 124 left, 130

Geoff Dann © FLL: 76 right, 77

Maayke de Ridder: 11 (Annet Doves & Hein Klemann), 13 (designer Tom Brekelmans), 21 right (designer Elspeth Thompson), 24 left (designer Elspeth Thompson); 25 (Nance van Norde), 28–9 left (Mahri and Simon Clutson); 63 (Ada van der Linden), 123 above (Ada van der Linden)

Kathryn Faulkner: 104–5, 113

Garden Picture Library/Howard Rice: 79

John Glover: 24 right, 45 right (designer Stephen Crisp), 72 (designer Jonathan Baillie), 73, 91 (designer Jonathan Baillie), 100, 106 above, 107 above, 107 below, 117 above (designer Susy Smith), 120, 123 below (painting by Tim King), 126 right–127 left (designer Jonathan Baillie)

Niccolò Grassi © FLL: 59 below, 86

Sunniva Harte: 39 below left (Giuliana de Conroy), 64 left (Paul Rippingale)

Jacqui Hurst © FLL: 57

Gavin Kingcome: 26 (courtesy of Raj and Sybil Kapoor, designer Christopher Masson), 30 above (courtesy of Raj and Sybil Kapoor, designer Christopher Masson), 37 (designer Cesca Maurice-Williams/The Urban Garden), 39 above (courtesy of Raj and Sybil Kapoor, designer Christopher Masson), 60–1 left (courtesy of Alistair McPhee), 70 (designer Matthew Dalby), 116–17 left (designer Del Buono Gazerwitz), 122 below (courtesy of Alistair McPhee), 124 right–125 (designer Haydee Softley)

Andrew Lawson © FLL: 59 above, 69, 76 centre, 85, 88, 89, 93 right

Sandra Lousada: 9, 43 below right

Eduardo Mencos: 27 right, 35, 74 right–75, 108

Clive Nichols: 22 (designer Wyniatt-Husey Clarke), 27 left (designer Charlotte Sanderson), 39 below right (designer Stephen Woodhams), 43 left (designer Wyniatt-Husey Clarke), 44, 52 (Candy Bros/Lighting Design International),

64 right–65 (designer Mark Brown), 83 (designer Charlotte Sanderson), 90 (Hedens Lustgard, Sweden), 96 (Vale End, Surrey), 99 (designer Wyniatt-Husey Clarke), 102–3 (Hedens Lustgard, Sweden), 106 below (Hedens Lustgard, Sweden), 112 (designer Christian Wright), 117 below (design Joe Swift and Thamasin Marsh), 119 right (Candy Bros/Lighting Design International), 121 (designer Nina Thalinson), 122 above (designer Christian Wright)

Emma Peios: 53

Gary Rogers: 7, 12, 19, 30–1 below, 31 above, 45 left, 50–1, 61 right, 62 left, 68, 78, 92 left, 98, 118–19 left, 127 below right, 128–9

Jane Sebire: 84 (designer Bernard Hickie)

Steven Wooster: 32–3 (designer Luciano Giubbilei), 43 above right (designer Michèle Osborne)

Author's acknowledgments

There are many people whom I would like to thank for helping with the writing and production of this book and making it such fun to do.

Firstly I want to thank Julie Apps who came up with the idea of a book on Pocket Handkerchief gardens. John Hare and my parents have always allowed me free rein to experiment in their gardens and many of the ideas in this book were tried out on them first. Sue Gibb has provided company on many garden visits, a nursery for my seeds and above all a wealth of knowledge preventing many horrendous horticultural blunders. Lucy Masters' enthusiasm and support right from the start made a huge difference and Paul Honour and Stephen Bankler-Jukes prevented disasters on the computer front. Donald Cameron and Fraser McKenzie provided a writing seat with a beautiful view, which may not have encouraged much work but was nevertheless lovely. Louy Carpenter, David Gibb, Chris Butcher, Parisa Ebrahimi, Mark Hammett and Mike Wood have all provided help at various stages for which I am very grateful.

As always my agent Teresa Chris has given me enthusiastic support and at Frances Lincoln I would like to thank picture editor Sue Gladstone, designer Caroline Clark and particularly my editor, Fiona Robertson, who dealt beautifully with my tendency to write too much and my inability to deal with any sort of technology.

Lastly, and most of all, I would like to thank Barry, who helped me see the potential of my tiny garden, read everything I wrote and encouraged me all the way.